Births

Births

William Saroyan, *1908—*

Introduction by
David Kherdian

 Creative Arts
Book Company
1 9 8 3

Copyright © 1983 by The William Saroyan Foundation
Introduction copyright © by David Kherdian

ISBN 0-916870-56-1 paperback
ISBN 0-916870-51-0 cloth

Library of Congress Catalog Card Number 82-73042

Printed in the United States of America

CREATIVE ARTS BOOKS
ARE PUBLISHED BY
DONALD S. ELLIS

Creative Arts Book Company
833 Bancroft Way
Berkeley, California 94710

Photo by Pennfield Jensen

Introduction

Saroyan, the poet of childhood, is dead.

He was my mentor, as I was for him, in our own loose relationship, the only pupil he ever had. To write an introduction for his last written book completes the circle, for he wrote the introduction to my first book. And titled it, too. I wanted to call it *A Family of Four*, but he suggested it be changed to *On the Death of My Father and Other Poems*. "The first is Tschaikovsky," he said, "the other is Beethoven. Start your career on the right note!"

Yes, he is gone, but a writer like Saroyan cannot die, and not only because of the writing but because of what he wrote about: childhood. And it is to childhood—and youth—that he returns us, because when I remember Saroyan I remember my discovery of him, which occurred long before we met—and I wonder if in fact that second (or *actual*) meeting was nearly as profound as the first meeting, when I met the writer, not the man—because in meeting the writer on his own turf (or page) I met my own mortality, my own need to have my mortality understood, and finally my own reason to seek continuance, with meaning, dignity and style. I think a writer, *our writer* does that for us, whether he means to or not. In struggling to find his own way to a kind of health and tolerance and grace and acceptance of the world, and again his own mortality, he permits us, in our joining, to seek this same possibility for ourselves. We feel, somehow, that our loves are on the line, and although we know that he has come through, we feel his struggle and ache, and know that he—perhaps alone—can feel ours, and is rooting for us, and yes, even helping us to find a measure of sanity and intelligence, without which it seems hopeless for us to go on.

This is what Saroyan meant to me, and this is what he meant to the generation that preceded and succeeded my own, and now because of certain conditions, the Saroyanesque magic and mystery that had infected so many of the young is no longer the phenomenon it was. His writing had a quality of innocence and eagerness and wonder about a moment—any moment of living—that made us feel more alive ourselves—more alive, that is, than we actually were, but for this very reason it made us yearn and stretch and seek a way to grow.

Perhaps these qualities cannot be summoned now because of these conditions, and perhaps it is this, and not Saroyan that has been taken from us, along with the feeling of expansiveness that the world and time of his making contained.

Saroyan belongs to youth, in the way that Thomas Wolfe and Dostoevsky and Salinger do. The best of his work, the early short stories, has too long been out of print. For these stories, full of the buoyancy of youth, and brimming with tough, uncompromising dignity and self-pride, have simply been pushed out of the larger arena of public affairs and need to be pushed back in, that the younger reader find Saroyan, as so many of us did in the past, and in finding him find themselves, as again so many of us did so long ago, but not so long ago that we have forgotten, or would ever care to forget.

— *David Kherdian*

Births

William Saroyan
74 Rue Taitbout 75009
Paris, France
Saturday, June 23, 1979 2 P.M.

A birth is a birth, and any human birth is the same as any other. It is anonymous, in short, and it might be said to be the birth of somebody supreme in the land of lore and legend, the son of God, that is to say, or the daughter of Heaven, and the mother might be said to be the mother of God. These are matters of words and sayings. There may be jokes about certain evil people not having been born, but the fact remains that if anybody is in a body he was born into it, and his birth was anonymous. After disagreeing that his father is God, no particular attention is directed towards his actual physical father, sometimes referred to as the biological father. He shot the sperm in the sport of love or confusion, and in the warm dark of the place it found its mark, and thus another person was begun instantly and three months short of a year was completed and forcefully ejected from the perfect universe, as unknown perhaps as the other, and probably not especially unlike it, who are we to say nay to that? Fathers are a dime a dozen, it's the mothers who count, and of whom we are certain. If in her traditional pain she drove Cain from his Eden, we know she is the mother, and we do not known who is the father, and it

2

has become fashionable to believe we ought to know, and to make a great deal of it. There are family trees, genealogy, and chronicles of begattings. It's fun and it tells us something, but a kind of something we know is really nothing at all, although I have marvelled about the family of Adams transplanted from England to New England—they are all such bright bastards we are almost compelled to believe there is something to the theory of human stock, and the improvement of it, although for several centuries, at least, all newfangled children have chosen their mates and thus their issue on the basis of something called love—which is at the very least a prevention of intelligence, and now and then even a perpetrator of crime, including murder. If a man doesn't love a woman but has issue by her, that issue ought to be reasonably right, while if a man loves a woman and loves her excessively and this comes to a birth, the party born may not be very much that might be considered lineal, inevitable, appropriate, expected, and satisfying. He might however be a genius, but it is more likely, much more likely, that he will contain the germ of genius that is carried forward half a million years and has one chance in ten billion, or something of that order. If royalty put forth a son, he may become one day the King, but there is no telling at birth who he really is, and what he might be said to be in common with others, a good fellow, a rotter, a calculator, a murderer, a gambler, a fool, or a diseased backgammon player. It doesn't matter, except that it does, and it is very very important. People not born kings or queens notice that fact, and it makes for a nagging of the soul. Or not born privileged, or rich, or handsome, and so on and so forth. There have been mothers who have remarked that they recognized genius in child the instant it was out, but we may suspect these people. If they are not exactly liars, they are also not concerned about lining up the full details in an acceptable way. There is surely some sort of statement from the breathing body of the newly emerged infant that might be presumed to tell us what we really want to know: and if we were skilled in the reading of that sort of statement we might know the entire life of that newborn one. If we knew that it was to be agony for eighty-eight years would we wish to spare the child and would we be justified in gently discontinuing its breathing in favor of a quick return to sleep? We would not, it would be murder pure and simple, just as it is said by some people, not friends of women, that if a foetus is stopped it is murder. We are not going to go into any of that, but we must observe that for every emergence from the womb there have been at least several zillion potentials which did not start at all. Was this any order of loss? Such loss is impossible, for during the years of humanity which are somewhat unknown in number and perhaps accurately unknowable, everybody has been born, and then born again, but not in the religious sense, although that happens (or not) to everybody sooner or later in one form or another. Right now we are concerned only about simple (very complicated) straight birth. And whoever it is, one fact alone is established: he came out, he breathes, he's on his way, and nobody knows who he himself really is, no matter what is known abut his mother or his father or his family tree or anything else. *2:25 P.M.*

5

William Saroyan
74 Rue Taitbout 75009
Paris, France
Sunday, June 24, 1979 1:15 P.M.

No man remembers his birth, although several liars have insisted that they do, and that they also remember their nine months in the womb, but let us understand that such talk is surely solely to amuse and confuse us, and perhaps it is intended to make us feel like fools because we remember nothing of the sort. As far as I know not even Laurence Sterne writing *Tristam Shandy* took it upon himself to say, or to have one of his people say, that he remembered his birth, and that it was quite an experience. His mother suffered, but it was not understood that her suffering was not nearly as great as his, and of another order, for there was pleasure of some sort or another in his mother's suffering and nothing but pain in his own, for he really did not want to be born, indeed he was absolutely outraged by the effrontery of herself imposing birth upon him instead of either not starting him at all, or keeping him safely home where he had been altogether satisfied to be. Laurence Sterne did not say any such thing, I am only saying what I believe he might have said, for he was a preacher, at last reports in one of the three or four dozen biographies written and published since his death, one or two of which have reached me, which I

6

have found fascinating, for he was not the kind of man who might readily be imagined as the man who was born to write *Tristam Shandy*. If you don't know that book, forget it, neither do I, although I have read around in it at least two dozen times. I do things by the dozens, I am sure you have noticed. Reading a book once is a brillant idea if you can see it through, and I can't. If I like the thing at all I want to be forever reading it, and if I don't like it, I'll be damned if I'll read more than enough to inform me that I don't like it. I have all the time in the world, as you do, too, but I cherish the miracle of writers and readers too much to spend any of that good time reading writing that I just don't like, that's all. And what sort of writing is it that I am sure I don't like? Well, I am not sure at all, but I don't seem to like to read any writing that is all wrought up about itself not liking itself and therefore wandering away into a continuing procedure of sickness—the taking of drugs, the rejection of girls and women in favor of boys and men, the enjoyment of self-debasement—is there such a word? debasement, wouldn't that be impossible: the fact that basement signifies that portion of a structure that is at the bottom, at the lowest level does however suggest that the word is related to self-humiliation and means something like the same thing. These are the people who in the parlance of the street shit on themselves, and in so doing somewhat shit upon their fathers and mothers, wives and children, friends and enemies, and thus upon all of us. They can do what they like of course, who can't? It is possible for anybody to have himself involved in a ritual of supreme absurdity, ending with his decapitation, for didn't it happen to a Japanese writer not so many years ago? And he believed in what he was doing. That is the part that makes us stop and wonder. Nothing is beyond being put into some kind of connection that, without justification, has meaning, or even a kind of heroics. He thought he was doing it for Japan, but there was nobody in Japan who really noticed that he had lost his head through the magnificent sword-work of a faithful admirer who was not himself beheaded or even tried for murder, or conspiracy to murder, and for all we know is now the happy father of quite a few sons and daughters in Tokyo. I find that I do not want to read the stuff of such crybabies, for that is the only name I seem to be able to find appropriate for them. What are they crying about? What are all the tears really for? Is it possible that when they came out, when they were born, they were somehow instructed that they must carry on in ways of self-hatred, one or two of them going even farther than the Japanese writer, going so far as to hope that in some kind of sexual pleasure they might be put to death—the opposite of birth, but perhaps with the sexual pain and pleasure of it—and then that they might be eaten. Think of it. These men want to be eaten. This is surely something that even a lobster doesn't really wish, although he might be said to have been born solely in order to make a fine meal for some human being somewhere, or even for some larger living creature either of the sea or the land— another order of lobster, for instance, a shark, a whale, a pelican, or a man on a desert island. I will not read these writers. Otherwise, I not only like to read, I have got to do so every day, and thank God for a writer like the preacher Laurence Sterne. *1:40 P.M.*

William Saroyan
74 Rue Taitbout 75009
Paris, France
Monday, June 25, 1979 11:45 A.M.

When a man dies he's named and known, and having given up the ghost the world is permitted to lock up his life, bring down the curtain, shut the door, or open the window, as you may choose, and anybody who wants to bother at all is free to consider his name, the events of his life as known and admired and dismissed as meaningless, or as loathed, or as suspected: he was born, he died, he went to Mexico from New York, he did some rather interesting geological work that turned out to be very profitable, but he was really not very interesting, although he amused some readers of newspapers by his reply to the question put to him by the correspondent of the New York Times, "Will you then consider running for President?" His reply was, "Who, me?" And he did not run. Silly stuff in short, but what can be said abut a man just born? Other than the simple facts of body and mother, for the Hebrew law does not consider the father at all, since he could very well be anybody. If the mother is Hebrew, the child is Hebrew, and never mind who the father is, or isn't. This is sensible, for many a man has pushed into many a woman, many a mother, and departed without fanfare, leaving the woman, the mother, to pass

10

along the easy theory that the infant's father is the mother's husband, and not some passing foreigner of God knows what people or religion? The mother starts, nurtures, and puts forth the child, and if the mother is Hebrew the child is Hebrew. Fathers do no such thing, although a variety of American playwrights have written about marriages among men and between the two of them some kind of child is brought into being, named, and given a place of honor in the arguments between the two men just as if one of them had given birth to real son, who was growing like the sons of mothers, and had a name and a character, just as each of the two men had, but this is unusual and at best a kind of cleverness which does not stand the test of time, for there is no living son (or daughter), and he is not at college, and he does not send telegrams asking for money, and he does not telephone to have them hear his voice. Women bear the children, and that's the end of the matter, and if men are ever going to go into that business, there has got to be a first time, as there recently was a first man to walk on the Moon, but so far there has been no such man. There have been many women who have been far more like men than their husbands or other men who have made them pregnant, but that is another matter entirely, and perhaps part of the reason why there have been entire large societies which have been matriarchical. Anybody who gives the matter any thought at all must come to the conclusion that being a man is a great convenience, at the very least, and that being a woman can at any moment become a great inconvenience, by reason of pregnancy, which may be the reason for the popularity among many women of getting to a nunnery. It cannot be said that the most interesting women of the world and history have not given birth, but there have been a very great number of women who haven't done that. They just haven't done it, for whatever reason it may have been, although one suspects that any women who hasn't given birth has not chosen this course but has had it happen to her—some women can't get pregnant, for instance, others can't bring a foetus to maturity, some are terrified of dying in childbirth and subconsciously compel miscarriages, and of course millions of women rid themselves of a new life by means of an abortion, amateur or professional, and this matter has become very meaningful to women struggling to become liberated from some of the inconvenience of being what they are—female and subject to pregnancy. The most ambitious man in the dimension of wishing to become his mother or some other female is able only to have Swedish and other surgery committed upon himself, upon his male genitals, and to take hormones which bring forward female breasts where lately there were male breasts, but none of this permits the man to conceive, nurture, and bear a child. What a blow that must be to many a man, for it is now clearly established that there are millions of such men all over the world, under every religious, political, and economic system—and in San Francisco they are organized into a political force and carry on like all similar groups. A clever novelist (and I'll be damned if I can think of who that might be, it is certainly not myself) would find it possible, most likely, to tell the hilarious story of a man who was buggered by an unknown man in a public lavatory only to find himself pregnant by some weird miracle possibly in the lower colon, and to give birth to a strapping eight-pound son—but think of the distinction of that boy: he is outrageously famous even before he has done anything at all on his own. *12:20 P.M.*

William Saroyan
74 Rue Taitbout 75009
Paris, France
Tuesday, June 26, 1979 1:00 P.M.

All right, the stage is set, the woman is ready, the midwife is ready, the foetus has long since moved a billion years through a billion variations of animal life and is a ripe and total entity, a body ready for breathing, for emergence into the light, for separation of the umbilical form the mother, for separation from everybody, for aloneness, for mobility, and after the more or less usual and predictable travail, out comes this fellow, so who is he? Nobody knows, that's all, so it is quickly attended to and shown to the mother, for in the mute language of vision she notices who it is: by God, he has it all, the genitals are there, and head and face and arms and legs and fingers and toes and the flawless miraculous neat nails upon them, and she smiles and thinks her private thoughts of course. It was so when it was Shakespeare, and it was so when it was Marx, and it was so when it was Cervantes, and it was so when it was Tolstoy, and it was so when it was Narek, and it was so when it was every last one of them who came out, and if I have restricted the names to that of boys who became men, and if this offends any female, any mother, any daughter, I regret the offense, it was not, it is not intended. For wasn't it herself who

14

received his incomplete portion and made it complete and unlike any other, ever, and nourished it and put it out in its time and place? When a new life is ejected from heaven or from nowhere, as you choose, it is always herself who has been delegated to do the ejecting, and this may very well be how it happens that women are able to be far more severe with their issue than men are, for men only plant the issue, and are forever after kindly disposed toward it, especially during its helplessness and its earliest years, when it is not really quite all there, insofar as occupancy of self and environment are concerned, hostile self and hostile environment, both. And when the arrival smashes all around the breather, what a noisy time that is. And if it is a lad who is actually Charles Dickens, nobody knows that fact, or wants to, and if it had been known perhaps the father would have thought, I really had in mind a chap not unlike myself, easy in his bones and not crowded out of his soul by all manner of worldly skill and smartness. And it was that very independence of his father that made Charles Dickens feel so poorly about his father, and about his own early years, although in comparison with the early years of many of the rest of us, he had much the best of it, for what is a little pasting of labels upon shoe-black bottles, or whatever the hell it was, in comparison with the things we were obliged to do for a penny or two. But Charley boy was a great crying fellow, and that is why he was also so funny, so really comic, such a laughter, such a believer in the validity of great expectations, and larky times ahead. But why did Charles Dickens become precisely only Charles Dickens? Is that perhaps the question? It is not the question at all, it most certainly is not the question, but on the other hand, come to think of it, perhaps it is the question, perhaps it is the very question, the only question, even though it compels us to quickly observe that it has no answer. We do not know. He might have readily have been Arthur Dickens, for instance, but there he is Charles Dickens. And so it was with so many of the other great Charleses, so to put it. Who will ever forget Chaplin, in the youth of genius, a fragile, delicate and yet indestructible and ferociously muscular fellow getting to the very center of the inevitable inseparableness of the sad and laughable—everything is ridiculous in life and in art, and this little Charley boy came along when moving pictures came along, and he took them over in their infancy and gave them very nearly their fullest identity. And what about Darwin, the lad with the high forehead, or so I am willing to suspect that he had. This Charles at birth was probably not recognizable at all, even by his mother, who very probably was only glad to have him embraceable rather than not, out rather than locked, and she had no idea that he would be the first human being to suspect who is born when a member of the human family is born, and that this exalted and miraculous fellow has come in a long line from all of the still-living and many long-gone forms of life, and during his gestation, as the word goes, in the womb of history and the womb of his own private life, at one point he wears a tail, the same as other animals, and finally loses it, and comes out tailless, or at any rate with only a concealed bone of the tail at the base of his spine. The great boys named Charles are many, but there are others who are named other names, too. *1:20 P.M.*

William Saroyan
74 Rue Taitbout 75009
Paris, France
Wednesday, June 27, 1979 11:40 A.M.

The son is the father's second chance, although he very seldom wants to be. There are exceptions, however. My cousin Kirk Minasian told me thirty or more years ago about his customers at a small grocery store patronised mainly by winoes on Grove Street near Laguna. I remember vividly the small man who told Kirk that as soon as he got home from work his large son would kneel down and demand that his father get on his back, whereupon the young man would solemnly carry his father in and out of all of the rooms of their apartment. It was a ritual of love, and the small father worshipped his son no less than his son honored him. I loved that story but never did it justice, although I mentioned it, somewhat in passing, in a story entitled "The Good Job," which I also made into a two-reel movie, in order to demonstrate to Louis B. Mayer that I should be the director of the story "The Human Comedy." The father who has not been to school is determined to get his son to college. This is especially true of the immigrant to America, for the leaving of the homeland in the first place was for improvement. The quarrels between fathers and sons are well-known (but alas not by me). Alexander (the

Great? Really? Did he permit such a fantasy?) went to a lot of trouble to demonstrate to his father (whose name I don't know, or don't happen to remember at this moment, was it Philip of Macedon?) that he, the son, was also a bigshot in the world of little, perhaps tiny, possibly invisible shots, and mounting his horse, he made the horse almost as famous as himself, which in itself suggest that there is exaggeration in the achievements of the great son. Kirk's brother Archie (but never Archibald) tells the story of another father who called his son to him and said, "Go mount horse and leave Chikawah Tribe. Go live among white man and great man." And then suddenly the father growls, "No mount horse *that* way." Edmund Wilson wrote earnestly of his different father, and I mention that tension between a father and a son because I read about it in the writing of the son, and have a few memories of Edmund Wilson himself that I find pleasant to have. Osbert Sitwell made his father into such a hilarious eccentric that one is obliged to suspect that the actual living man himself, the father himself, was sure enough eccentric enough but that the son in writing about him was having fun. But surely these are not classic examples of the secret expectations of fathers about their sons, and I shall not be likely to summon forth such examples, for I do not work that way. I do not look things up in reference books. Indeed I don't look up anything anywhere, although I know that the big-money writers pay good wages to researchers, the same as corporations, but the writers bore me even more than the corporations and their executives do. They wear pointy shoes, highly polished, and I have never been able to believe a man who wears such shoes, polished by a private slave, is anybody I ever want to know anything more about, writer or corporation executive, father of sons or father of daughters, for what is it that a calculating clever writer wants in a son, and what could a corporate executive ever imagine he would really enjoy noticing that his son had become? Does this mean then that only I and my kind are ever likely to be promising fathers? That would be ugly, but even so, that is precisely what this means. And what kind is this kind? Comic, out of the fullest possible awareness of the inevitable absurdity of human life, whatever life in bears and salmon may be. Perhaps ants and bees may be said to live meaningful lives, or at any rate well-ordered lives, but the procedure by which they, and termites and other kindred forms of life, come into being, from a huge swollen surely insane common mother, alienates their potential order and meaning away from human ideas of such things and keeps them in a dimension of monotony, repetition, and madness which is the consequence of preposterous and horrible sanity. And of course there are mothers who having failed to become movie queens push their daughters as they had been unable to push themselves, and now and then the daughters become great stars, and very difficult to abide, out of context. So long as they perform parts and somebody beholds them in action they may be said to be tolerable, but as themselves they are not quite acceptable, for they are not actually real. The question is, how did it ever happen that fathers and mothers came to believe they ought to have a second chance outside of themselves? *12:10 P.M.*

William Saroyan
74 Rue Taitbout 75009
Paris, France
Thursday, June 28, 1979 12:45 P.M.

It must amuse each of us, and God, and Eternity, and the Sun, and the Eye, and the Ear, that we are forever hitching ourselves back to the strange connection with God, and Eternity, and everything else, by means of the first event of world, if private action. That is the birth of each of us. I was amazed long ago when my son, then twenty, wanted to know at what hour of the day or night I was born, so that at Grand Central Station in New York, at a cost of one dollar in U.S. Currency, he could get my full astrological reading from a machine. I was fascinated by this transaction, and not having the facts, pieced together what I did seem to have gathered from the mother herself, and her mother, chatting and overheard by me. Well, it was a Monday about ten or eleven at night, and my mother's kid brother was in the house on Eye, or I Street, later called Broadway, near Ventura Avenue in Fresno, and he was cracking jokes, as the saying is, until finally my mother, about to give birth to her fourth, and last child, herself aged twenty-six, her first born having arrived when she was just past sixteen, ordered him out of the house and the appropriate quietude was established, the mother and daughter chatted along as they

22

always did, and the midwife, also in the family, a second cousin called Osko, or perhaps the sound of it will be made more possible if the spelling is Ohskoh, older than my mother's mother, who was about fourty-four, the midwife joined them in the easy talk of life in Bitlis, other births, and marriages and husbands and my father Armenak, at that moment at rest in a vineyard worker's barracks at Droge's vineyard near Sanger, about twelve miles east of the house on Eye Street. And a good thing, too, for he was a preacher, a poet, and not to put too fine a point upon it, a fool, a failure, and totally tortured by the literal Christian admonition that a man must be truthful and charitable and good and must love his enemies. Well, my father's enemies were members of his own family, to whom he used to refer as the noble ones, the righteous ones, because they were actually the opposite and ferociously so, and very successful in the world, and rich. But of course I told my son I couldn't be sure that it wasn't until after midnight that I was born, and consequently the day was now Tuesday, September 1, 1908. Even so, he said, and I put the currency into the machine which began to grind and groan and after about four minutes a long sheet of paper, in four or five foldings, came out of the machine, and my son picked it up eagerly and indeed with some excitement, and began to read the rather purple print as if he was finding out all about his father, saying as he went along such things as wow or hey. We went up to Forty-second Street and into the big Automat and took coffee and doughnuts to a table, around eleven at night, and he read the whole thing to me and commented upon everything, and as he did so I had to think, For God's sake, is my son feeble-minded, or what? He really believes this shit. He thinks it is all in the stars, and that suggests that he is not quite willing to select his own character out of what he has, and his own health and his own usage of his raw material in the making of his identity. Is he, then, not unlike my father, his grandfather? And when we said so long that night and I went up to my room at the Royalton Hotel, at Forty-four West Forty-fourth Street, room 1015 looking directly across the street at the upper floors of the Algonquin Hotel whose rates were about twice as high as those at the Royalton, and whose rooms were about half as large, I got out the machine astrological reading and tried to read it, but it was impossible. All I could think was, What the hell's going on with my son? Is he looking for excuses not to accept the hard work for years and years without which he cannot be most fully and meaningfully himself? Is he looking for alibis for being a stupid pot-smoking frightened absurd man, aged twenty? Is he looking for justification for not making any demands of himself at all, and for making enormous demands of me, his father, and at the same time finding enormous fault with me, which I came to be out of muscle in body, mind, and spirit. Where's his muscle? But having thus given myself in this recitation the best of it all, having made my son out a fool, surely the fool that he is, and having made myself out not a fool, I must return to the point I am trying to make. Birth is the point from which we derive the means of doing whatever we may find it impossible not to do, and that point involves the mother, and the father, and all of the lore and culture that may be in them, or part of them, and so we are forever going back to the event as if that birth was not really especially unlike the birth of Jesus the son of God. *1:10 P.M.*

William Saroyan
74 Rue Taitbout 75009
Paris, France
Friday, June 29, 1979 12:45 P.M

If you ask somebody what he may have heard about his very first moments of life, speaking as a small boy with his mother, he is likely to look at you as if you had asked a very strange question, for almost nobody has ever gone into the matter of his earliest breathing, his earliest encounters with that connection with everything, the drawing of breath, and his earliest putting up with both the external and the internal, the outside and the inside, air and place and people, and himself inside all alone. There have surely been many who heard a few words about the actual arrival out of the great place, perhaps the greatest of all, if still uncharted, unknown, and still unconnected with what it must very probably be the map of, so to put it, beyond measure, especially if the mother nearly perished during the event, and is remembering it in a little idle conversation with her mother and the one whose difficult emergence nearly killed the mother happens to be within hearing distance, and senses or knows that it was himself who is being referred to. And what does it mean to him? More mystification, more not knowing, more helplessness about what happened—and now it is all gone, there is no way for him to

26

know what that was all about, although the consequence of it was that he was deposited upon the floor of the world or at the center of history, or the universe that is lighted by the sun, and that he is now on his way into the future, instant by instant, all of it not understood, and that his end is somewhat predictable, for he has both heard about and sensed the end, he has not died but others have, and he has experienced deathliness in the form of wrongness, of sickness, of fever, of treacherous conditions inside himself as body and as spirit both. But now and then somebody comes along and says that his first moments of mortality were absolutely delightful, and we imagine that he must be a liar or a very imaginative soul, but who can say that this is not the very truth about all who have ever been born, and are still moving toward the end, or long long arrived there and died. The evidence seems to be from the way bodies move in all creatures that there is something like joy in the condition of having life. It is a desperate joy, then, because the body and its spirit know that the occupation of substance charged with energy and the unknown future has got to be more connected to failure than to success, and indeed that every success is a form of failure, and in emerging there has actually been the opposite of emerging, there has been a confirmation of deeper disappearance— but no, this won't do, language is too supple and too eager and willing to serve any purpose it is asked to serve. What the writer is saying is actually this, most likely: we don't know even the few little unimportant details that we have carefully documented and believe we do know. We just don't know anything at all about ourselves, perhaps because we are not ourselves, we are not the infant just out of the womb, and on its way into the world, which we do not know at all, which we imagine that we have made, have imposed upon the earth, but really have done something else entirely, perhaps we have made a toy or a monument or a game of some kind, but whatever it is that we do not know, and whatever it is that we do know, or believe we do, whenever we do something, it is surely actually something else, so that when the man embraces the woman, and they put themselves together, and dance inwardly to this help-less rhythm of release and change for each, which turns out to be the starting in the woman of a new life, that is not in fact what has happened at all. Something else has happened which for all these millions of years we have failed to notice or even to suspect or to know, and the reason for this may very well be that it is none of our business, as the saying is. Our business seems to be to be ignorant and helpless even while we believe our knowledge is becoming enormous and our control is well-established and right if not righteous. And these are of course fantasies pure and simple, and yet what can we do, we have tried everything we have been able to think of as possibly helpful, and always we have finally noticed that we have again been deceived, and possibly self-deceived, although the self part of the deception is itself a deception for there is no self, there is only nature's use of the illusion of it not just in human forms of life, or animal, but in microscopic forms, and very probably also in forms that seem dead, or static, such as stones. And yet we have come forth as a consequence of the existence for billions of years of light—and light suggests beholding and knowing, and yet it were actually as if we had emerged from one darkness into a greater darkness. *1:05 P.M.*

William Saroyan
74 Rue Taitbout 75009
Paris, France
Saturday, June 30, 1979 11:50 A.M.

Whenever I go to work at a new piece of writing which I
know is going to involve daily work for thirty or more days,
sometimes ninety days, and now and then one hundred, or
more probably one hundred and one, in the tradition of the
Armenian and Persian East, I do no research of any kind at
all, I have nobody help in any way, whether secretary,
typist, editor, or friend, who might be invited to read some
of the new writing and to remark what he thinks of it and
how he feels it might be improved. I speak of all this because
it is common procedure for apparently all writers, or at any
rate most of them, for if I proceed without any of that
business and clutter it must follow that there are other
writers who proceed in the same way. But if I am put in
touch with somebody or other in a social way I may direct
the conversation into an area from which I might learn
something I want to have ready for usage, if that becomes
desirable. At La Varenne night before last I met a young
teacher of history at one or another of the American
colleges that have branches, so to call them, in or around
Paris, and I said, Well, let me ask you if in your studies you
have ever heard of a birth that was not anonymous, totally

immersed in mystery, excepting of course births in royal families, for there is an established procedure with them that announces title-to-come, the firstborn to become king in time, in short. Have you heard of a birth that for some reason compelled everybody, not just the mother and father, to know that this infant was Erasmus, for instance, and I must remark that I am amused by the fact that I used that name, for I know nothing at all about Erasmus, although I suspect that he was born, and that the event took place in olden times, as the saying goes, and that he might very well have been a scientist who made very significant discoveries about the universe, the action of the sun and the design of the many planets in space, or that he was some kind of philosopher. And I did not remark that I found philosophers pleasant to read not for what they talked about at great length, but for the manner in which they talked. I can't read Sartre, at all, for instance, and as far as Existentialism is concerned, like all other philosophical theories, inventions or discoveries, it turns out to be something any infant or small child who is not demented or shortchanged in the soul knows virtually by instinct. And

31

just the following morning I saw a snapshot of Sartre in *Le Figaro* or some other Paris paper standing beside, or beneath, a large young man, who was holding Sartre by the elbow, both to protect and to guide him, and at first glance I thought Sartre must be the boy's grandmother. Do philosophers have that inclination—to become grandmothers? The history professor replied that no, he did not know of anybody outside of royalty who might be said to be a known person. I said, Is there no lore at all about anybody? Mohammed, for instance? Or Shakespeare? Did not somebody look at Shakespeare when he was four hours old and say, This is him, this is he, this is the great one? And the young professor indicated by a smile and a slight shake of the head, negative, that he knew of no such event, and so when the Master Teacher at that famous cooking school called out, Ah table, we sat down and began to eat a ten course haute cuisine dinner that the twelve students, mainly American, including the professor's wife, had cooked—but not quite flawlessly. There was something off about every dish served, but the long table seating all of the students and almost as many husbands and friends was busy with eating and talking, but I don't think I shall be quickly willing to go there again for a free meal, because if the cuisine is going to be haute I would like to be able to predict that it is going to be authentic haute. Great cooks, great chefs are born, as we know, just as great and ungreat of all other categories are born, but as far as I am concerned the best food for me is the plain food of the Saroyan family, of Bitlis, of Fresno, and I am equal to the fixing of enough of these dishes to satisfy the best hunger I am likely ever to have. I spoke about this to the master chef and teacher who sat directly across from me at the table. I like very plain food most of the time, I said. And that includes Eisbein, which is a steamed knuckle of the pig, with sauerkraut, mashed potatoes, and beer. I find this German peasant's dish very satisfying, but once on the North German Lloyd Flagship *Bremen* the astonished waiter said he might be able to find some sauerkraut and frankfurters, but no pig's knuckle. The Chef said, "Oh, good eating does not have to come from haute cuisine." Indeed, I thought, it comes only from health and hunger. *12:15 P.M.*

William Saroyan
74 Rue Taitbout 75009
Paris, France
Sunday July 1, 1979 12:00 P.M.

What is a birth? How different is a human birth from a non-human one? Is the mystery of what a human birth probably is the consequence of a similar or even identical mystery of the birth of a bear, for instance? Are there dangerous and even deadly complications of parturition among animals, as there certainly are among humans? And let us never permit ourselves not to honor the female of our kind by keeping in mind that when we speak of human birth we mean out of the female half of the human race alone, however vulnerable this emphasis may make us to ribald jest. Women alone bear the human race, not just sons and daughters of the male half of that race. They bear the whole race, and this bearing, this burden, this privilege or this condemnation if you will, is universal among women, and no matter who an individual woman might be if she is willing, or if she is the victim of an accident of behavior, if a consequence overtakes her from play, plan, program, preference or whatever, it is she, and not he, her adored and tolerated partner, who must suffer the time it takes for her to be transferred from a light and lissome human being into a life-manufacturing factory whose procedures are mute,

34

dark, and impossible to understand beyond the superficial and obvious established simple facts of them. She is to be put out and not he. And after an enormous amount of racial ancient time, ages of time, and a not inconsiderable amount of immediate time, about nine months, about 280 days, give or take, of terrible discomfort, of humiliation, even, of distortion of physical self, of risk and fear and possibly terror, the time comes, and the manufactured product is forced out of the woman, a whole thing, except for the cutting of the cord that nourished and bound him to the poor woman, or if the finished product is not forced out by the woman seeking to be restored to herself again, she seeks to force him out, and both of them find that they are helpless about being forced and about forcing. It is understandable that apparently most women have accepted their role as the mothers of the human race, for you do not go to a lot of trouble to protest that which is the simple fact of life, of continuity, of procedure. And in accepting that role of motherhood and of performing that preposterous work, it is also understood that a large portion of sanctification will be placed about the accepting of the role and of beauty about

35

the performing of it. Is any of this, however, really valid, really justified, or is there simply a natural piece of comfort in it, from heaven, from God, from mystery, from tides and cycles, from nature? Well, of course only human beings have the capacity to make of any piece of business what they will, and birth has been made into such a vast sanctification that when a woman until very recently found herself caught, pregnant, but did not want to suffer the time-taking and possibly terrifying procedure of manufacturing the product, unknown to her, or from knowledge of the male involved; undesirable, or even terrifying, soul-destroying, sickening, deadening, as it would be if the male was a monster of one sort or another, or insane, or deformed, or diseased, or her father, and wanted the pregnancy prematurely terminated her desire appeared to be unacceptable to both men and women who had no knowledge of the truth but felt that if she ended the pregnancy she would commit murder. This still goes on, as we know of course, and not for reasons of very much more than the wish of a woman simply not to bother because she preferred to devote her body, herself, to other activities, and also because she was not a wife in a home, for instance, or because she was a wife in a home with a husband and already too many children to properly manage, or because she needed time to think about the whole business of being, of being a woman, of being captured by that ultimate meaning, and about her possible usages of that meaning, or her avoidance entirely of that aspect of her identity. Well, what is a birth, then? The answer is that it is somewhat that which the woman involved has had imposed upon her, and her thinking and feeling, by centuries of custom, superstition, religion, race, as well as her own private incommunicable connection to perhaps large, possibly vast and very complex things and actions which she senses but does not understand: and all of these come together into the form of the fantasy: This one is the one. This is he, this is the one we have all been waiting for. But why couldn't it be, This is she? We don't know, but it seems to be the consequence of simple choice between the two sides of the human race, and the male was chosen. *12:35P.M.*

William Saroyan
74 Rue Taitbout 75009
Paris, France
Monday, July 2, 1979 11:30 A.M.

Somebody has said that the human race can't be presumed
to be a dismal mistake, a fiasco, a sad accident when one
takes into account that in a comparatively short time (to the
universe a billion years, the saying goes, is a lot like a second
on a ticking watch) the human race has produced Mozart.
This makes sense, at least of a certain order, for if the five
hundred million people of the world at the time of Mozart's
birth were not collectively his father and mother, we are
obliged to observe that his father and mother were in
noway, or nowise, especially unlike all of the others, and so
it was the human race which had put him forth, by way of
Mr. Mozart and through the channel of Mrs. Mozart. This
ought to be acceptable to the most disputatious person, but
it probably is not. Mozart, he might insist, came from God,
not from the human race. Such disputants need to be
respected, but not excessively, as many disputants are, not
excluding Luther, who was also produced by the whole
human race. What did Mrs. Mozart believe when she
became pregnant and the pregnancy proceeded and the
foetus went through its mystic rites until it became a full
living breathing body in the womb, and was then put out,

and became the maker of the music that so many human beings feel helps to make the human race tolerable, helps to make it seem to be a benign not a malignant accident of cells and tissue and procedures that to this day are beyond understanding, no matter how we try. There is no such enthusiasm and indeed gratitude about much more historic and active men (and women), such as Genghis Khan, Alexander, Napoleon, and so on, although there is a continuing fascination about them. They did public things, exterior things, but Mozart, like all artists, did private interior things, that nevertheless were always directed to everybody else, however difficult it might be for the gift to be accepted by anybody at all beyond the confines of the family, or the concert hall, always restricted to an assemblage of musicians, a conductor of music, and several others, such as a publisher. An orchestra was the means of making Mozart's music something real, or literally the means of transferring it from silence to sound, and to structured and appealing sound. The historical men were virtually bereft of any interior connection with the development of the soul in man, and Mozart was connected to that soul in a way that permitted him and surely compelled him to say things in harmonious sounds progressing to a new silence at the conclusion of the Mass, or whatever it might be, which nobody else had ever said, and which no other order of communication, as the overused word has it, could be capable of, although written, spoken, declaimed, and read language could very probably go as far as musical sounds, provided a Mozart of writing came along, and he did of course soon enough in Shakespeare—unless of course Will wrote his stuff before Wolf began to compose his, it doesn't really matter, for the point is that each was brought forth by a woman—this cannot be disputed—by means of a man, this can be disputed just in case several men may have put sperm inside a woman during a few days before conception. We may presume that Mr. Mozart impregnated Mrs. Mozart and that it was not another man, and we have always been willing to accept that the same situation was true in the Shakespeare household. But even if the sneak had been the one, the situation would be the same—the entire human race alive at that time would need to be regarded as the parents of these wonder boys. It is just too much for a nice sensitive woman, the mother perhaps of a variety of other boys and girls, to give birth to Mozart or Shakespeare as if it were only herself who had done it. And of course no mother of such infants knows who they are when they arrive, or how to account for them after they have begun to give to the whole human race the gifts that are unaccountably in them and necessary to pass around. I have never heard of a great poet, for instance, who kept his poems to himself, for the pleasure of only God, but it is not altogether inconceivable that an enormous individual of this order did indeed write a great body of poetry which never reached the human race. As nature taught us to remark, There's plenty more where that came from. Is it nature, then, that has done it all, and is doing it all? Well, we needn't quibble, but if it is not nature alone, it is certainly nature also, with surely a variety of elements and actions not known. *11:55 A.M.*

William Saroyan
74 Rue Taitbout 75009
Paris, France
Tuesday, July 3, 1979 3:50 P.M.

We get born, don't we. Whoever we are, we get ourselves born, don't we? How in the world did it happen to each of us? We were in no way involved and yet it did happen and it turned out to be that each of us was the one who was born. It is something to think about, most likely. How did it happen? What were the odds against it? Billions of billions, were they not? And yet there it is, and there we are, there we were, inside and ready and coming out and out, and it was surely something like death, like becoming done instead of becoming started, and yet it did happen to us, it did not happen to our brothers and sisters, it was the beginning of each of us, and we have never understood it, we have always taken it for granted. A male and a female get together and between them they feel something and do something and after the usual time a birth happens, and who it happens to is never known, and after a long time it is still not known, and then death happens, and neither he nor they the male and the female know what happened or how or really why, but a great deal therefore is made of when.

42

Well, are we then acts of faith, do we get ourselves born out of the faith of our mothers and fathers that we want to be born, that we will live good lives, or does it happen out of ignorance and helplessness in them? Well, whatever it is, whatever the answers may be, what it comes to is that there are almost a thousand million of us in China alone, and a great number in India, in Russia, in the countries of Africa, in North America, in South America, in the Islands of the Pacific, and everywhere where there is earth enough on which we may stand and walk, there we are, and it began by birth. It is a marvel of some kind, perhaps the greatest marvel of all, but there are wise people who are saying birth is happening to too many of us, and that soon there won't be earth enough for everybody to stand and walk upon, or food growing out of the earth, for everybody to eat, and all the rest of that tiresome talk. So what? Is that not the answer that must be made to the people who are sounding warnings—cut it out. No more births. Enough. More than enough. Stop. Drop dead. Quit while you are ahead of the game. And yet always always we get ourselves born, don't we. It is something we know nothing about at all, and yet it happens to us all the time. We do not happen to birth, birth happens to us. We ought to find out a little something or other about this. Who are we? Why are we getting ourselves born this way these many billions of years, what is it that we expect is to come from this compulsion we have to come into the possession of matter charged with mystery and movement? Well, who knows, who knows? It just seems to go on and on, and soon we are on our way to school, brooding about the whole thing, and wishing, wishing something, wishing something better, something more, and trying to imagine what it is that we wish for, and if we will ever find out, and if we do find out, will we know how to get it and have it, or will it turn out to be another one of us who has somehow gotten himself born out of our never having understood how it had happened to us. *4:00 P.M.*

William Saroyan
74 Rue Taitbout 75009
Paris, France
Wednesday, July 4, 1979 4:15 P.M.

What is it that we like so much about disorder? It is freedom, isn't it? The deliverance from the oppression of keeping things right and straight, sensible and useful, and the hunch, very probably, that in disorder there is this best order of order, if we may put it that way. For there does seem to be a natural push of energy in the direction of disorder, of freedom, of not being obsessed with details, of being open-minded and open-spirited about the probability that our compulsion to keep things in good order is destructive of a higher keeping of order, to the end that something more desirable might come into being. This feeling which may not be uncommon, really, even to those people most famous for rigidity in such matters as establishing and maintaining order, such as the Teutons, let us say, however inaccurate this may turn out to be, comes very possibly out of the disorder about the procedure of starting and nurturing and putting forth a new human being alive and with his character, identity, and even destiny secretly if carefully tucked away inside the mystery somewhere, a vast disorder brought down and put into any pregnant woman's belly: she doesn't know what is happening to her, and to the

46

new life, and her partner, beside her and established as an identity and even as a participant in the mystery, or gone, or unknown, as in the births that attend the passing of an Army through a village, town, city, or nation, as one may presume was commonplace during the Crusades, with a rather fascinating if confusing change imposed upon the local character insofar as biological differentiation might be said to be concerned—and it is a confusion and it isn't. For high up in the Caucasus where the Ungush people persist, descendants of English crusaders, there is upon all these people the character of the Caucasus upon all its children, and while many of the Ungush might readily be presumed to be the descendants of brave English boys going to the rescue of Christianity from the Turks and the Arabs and other Moslems, in Jerusalem, or to the rescue of Jesus himself, there is in fact almost nothing else than fair skin and blue or pale eyes in the Ungush and nothing of London limey or Oxford don or Scotch lord in them. They came out of a larger womb than that of the unique and special female which received the charge of life from the passing Englishman, and this womb was the Caucasus itself, for the songs

47

about anybody's birthplace and place of childhood if not indeed of all of his mortal time and activity liken that place to womb, mother, and milk of breast, with such ferocious devotion to all of this mystic melange of deeply felt but surely misunderstood and yet vitally real lore that in time of combat upon neighbor, in time of war, all the braves, so to call them, all of the males stir themselves out of their boring and deadening torpor and stupor of peace and complacency, and facing death with a joyous gladness swear to drive off the intruder, or perish. And how many times it has happened, and how important it has been to all peoples and lores, and what profound pride it has compelled, mingling with sorrow and joy. Until now at last the foolishness of it all is becoming impossible not to notice because there can be no such war any more, no such misconception about place and culture, about combat and risk, about victory or failure, about the inflicting of death upon the enemy, or having it inflicted upon the self—because no such combat is any longer possible. It is now very vast combat with such withering destructiveness that there is no time for mistaken sentiment, bravery, confusion, singing, self-deceiving, prancing about, transforming of the self from individual to insect-like member of a mob. All that is out, dead and gone—or it is preserved deliberately as if to permit a continuation (in small wars) of the lies that were so comfortable for so long in a supreme kind of orderliness on behalf of the majestic disorderliness of a life coming into being in a womb for eviction and arrival into a dimension of openess, of air, of the pneumatics of connection with secret and nonsecret procedures of growth and the private endurance and exploitation of time, in units of day and night, of four seasons, of sun-time and moon-or-night-time, and of wakefulness and life or sleep, and dream, and if not death then something not yet discovered or identified. This disorder, this celebration of danger and death, has been useful because it was well within bounds for centuries, and permitted freedom. *4:35 P.M.*

William Saroyan
74 Rue Taitbout 75009
Paris, France
Thursday, July 5, 1979 5:15 P.M.

What kind of a foetus were you? Certainly this might be reasonably considered a valid question for anybody engaged in the business of trying to understand a murderer, a bigtime robber, a liar, a mischief-maker, an arsonist, a planter of bombs in bus stations or in foreign legations, or on the other hand a writer of a very great poem, or play, or story, or even letter to the President, for there are writers whose form is only the letter, and only to the President, or the best graffiti on the wall of a great bridge in great letters, something for instance along the lines of No, for heaven's sake, no—and let the racing motorist try to imagine the rest of the beseechment. As it is, extraordinary people, destructive as well as productive, tend to be asked something like what sort of a child were you? And of course the implication is that the child is the father of the man. If that's so, then might it be considered to imagine that the foetus is the mother of not only the woman but of the man as well. How far back are we invited to go in order to hope to understand ourselves—that is to say, if we feel the need of this sort of thing urgently or even violently, and there are surely as many people who do not need to understand themselves, as

50

there are who do, at least now and then. Sigmund Freud who has captured the imagination of the human race of the West did not feel he needed to understand himself, at least not excessively, or how may we justify his openly asking, What do they *want*? That is to say, what do women want? What did his wife want, his mother, his sister, his daughter, his mistress, the whores he may or may not have patronised, the women with whom he tried to chat at parties. What he was asking may very well deserve to be carefully studied, from all sides. Is it first of all an insult to half the human race, at the outset? It would seem to be. Is it also an insult to the male half of the human race for such a large mind as that of Sigmund Freud to be reduced to the kind of desperation that one tends to associate only with very angry young men madly in love whose women are as a matter of fact not quite sure that they *do* want, for a vast number of reasons, not excluding the simple one that the choice at that time is still open—there could be another man who might be more desirable. Is the question stupid? Especially in that if it can be asked, it follows that the asker must consider why he has asked it, and try to find out how he has failed to understand his women at least well enough not to be driven to an emotional outburst but to feel they are justified in finding their unique position in the scheme of things not especially easy to take, and the basic cause of a profound and nagging discontent, so that (in some of them all of the time, and in all of them some of the time) there seems to be no living with them. And there he was, the discoverer of the sick soul in the human race, especially in women, and there he was using sleep, using dreams to suggest to him the probable reason for their sickness and unhappiness and even temporary insanity, or whatever anybody might care to call it. And he looked the original wise man, he did not look like a young lover, he sucked at his cigar, and he grew his beard, and he discussed the human soul with his colleagues, he made enemies of many of them, and he wrote a kind of prose that was as good as any written by professional novelists of the first order, and somewhere along the line he asked the famous question about women, and apparently believed the question was restricted to women, and was not also to men, including enormous men like himself, the great innovators of science, in his case, rather than religion or art, although these things were by no means out of the science he worked in. He wanted his cigar, and got it, and his beard, and his respect, and the honors bestowed upon him, and elegant opposition of his peers, and was served hand and foot by his wife and children, and by pretty much everybody else, and got it, got it all, but was never even tempted to ask, why do I insist that I must have all of this honor and adulation? What's the matter with me? What sort of a small boy was he, after he had been the kind of foetus he had been? When did he discover that his best chance to be somebody was to forget sports, music, trade, and set out on his own into a whole brandnew or long neglected dimension of human thought? Might not a good teacher of equestrianism in Vienna throw up his hands in despair, and cry, What is it that Sigmund wants? Why can't he sit a horse? Why is he so inferior, so weak, so spoiled? *5:55 P.M.*

53

William Saroyan
74 Rue Taitbout 75009
Paris, France
Friday, July 6, 1979 1:30 P.M.

Is the first breath of man, of the continuing man, a crying out of sorrow or is it a crying out of joy? Well, it certainly sounds as if this new party, all red and total, whatever his fate is to be, in the next minute, hour, year, decade, or perhaps a whole century, it certainly sounds as if his crying out is in sorrow, for nobody has suggested as far as I know that the crying out is laughter, but now I do suggest that that is what it actually is, so that at least a dispute about the entirety of human life might be inaugurated, and perhaps a new attitude come into being about the sound of the crying out, and the implications of that sound insofar as reaching a decision about its meaning is concerned. Reader, old friend, you and I, we are a couple of idiots, now, aren't we? For here I am writing what I am writing and here you are (and God knows when, or where) reading it, and it is surely absurdity that is involved here. The newborn infant cries, he does not laugh. That is what the world has decided on, and nobody so far has disagreed, because the evidence seems to be indisputable, but I come along a billion years later, walking in a very easy manner into the arena, and I dispute the whole thing. Gentlemen, I say, fathers, ladies, I say, mothers,

54

listen to me, please: your children have all come into life, form, mystery, and presence inside the physical limits of the human body, male or female, in gladness, with laughter. They have not come into this experience in sorrow and in weeping. That has been an error of interpretation pure and simple, and I would like to suggest to the United Nations that immediate steps be taken to improve the quality of all of the interpreting that has been going on in that august body since its founding in San Francisco in the middle 1940s, and its continuation ever since, doing nothing but good every day and all the way. To the United Nations Organization, then, I say, Keep at it, boys, stick to it, girls, you are doing a fine job, but now the time has come to look into the matter of the full depth and breadth of potential interpretations, and so let us start with the first breath of man repeated a thousand times a minute in all of the world when women deliver themselves, or are delivered by divine procedure, of their burdens and glories, in human life continuing. Popular theory has that the child's announcement of health and full commencement is in the form of weeping, and here I am putting forward the theory that that theory is the consequence of very limited literalism and very inferior usage of intelligence and imagination, because the outburst of sound which is a confirmation that the new one has geared itself into time and humanity is not a cry of sorrow, it is a piece of helpless laughter, as when a great clown or comedian is so powerful at his work that he does not permit strong men to stop their helpless laughter and he compels even old and wise women to wet their pants with the simple pleasure of their enjoyment of his absurd but delightful belittlement of God, nature, truth, universe, and mystery with all of its wealth lying in darkness, limitless and impossible to light up. I say the babies, the infants, the newcomers are latched onto themselves and ourselves with such astonishment, shock, surprise, and simple if overwhelming pleasure that they must laugh, some of them in roaring sounds, others in tiny almost silent sounds, only their little red faces twisting with the hilarious comedy of their good and totally unexpected good fortune. I say that. What say you, reader? If you say "bullshit, sir," then of course we do not become instant enemies, although I am just a little disappointed both in yourself, sir, madam, young lady, young man, boy, girl, and in your choice of word. You might have said, "Doubtful," and I would have considered how civilized you really must be. But all right, let us not quibble, we are forever quibbling in the Western World, a couple of dry-nose faggots started it, Socrates and Plato, let's call them, and ever since it is unavoidable that in idle talk even, human beings quibble about the details of vastness. You may say my theory is a poor one, I say it is a good one. Indeed I say it is a great one, and if the truth is told it is irrefutable. I believe that irrefutable means that you can't expose it as a falsehood, or misconception of some kind. The newborn's first breath segues into laughter for the simple reason that it is in us, his father and mother, and their fathers and mothers, and the whole shooting-gallery of us that experiencing mortality is quite a comic thing, and that no matter how really rotten most of the human experience is, there are always the jokes, and they are so funny nobody can possibly not laugh, starting with the red-face red-ass newborn little bastard. *1:50 P.M.*

William Saroyan
74 Rue Taitbout 75009
Paris, France
Saturday, July 7, 1979 1:15 P.M.

I was sitting in the Gillis Branch of the Fresno Public Library one afternoon in the year 1978 I believe it was, when I came upon a review in Time Magazine for a book by somebody whose name I read and instantly forgot, for it had all the force of such a name, and in a separate box, not far from the review, was a long list of names of the greatest members of the human race of all time. This sort of thing earns money for a cheap publisher and a smart writer, and I am all for it, I love non-books, for they do tell us how much we have to be thankful for in coming upon a book that is a book now and then, and in any case the book written by somebody rather well-known by the public through newspapers, radio, television and gossip, but actually not written by him, at all, written with, as the money-hustling publisher calls it, Daniel M. Willingfertig, so that you will pay more attention to the name of the famous man, printed enormous in any case, while the name of the man who actually wrote the silly and fascinating book of a nice blend of atrocious and pathetic lies and absurd and really horrible truths (but always between the lines), such a book which is invented or produced by a publisher or a non-publisher is called, at least

58

in the trade, a non-book, and it is always entertaining, if in a rather extraordinary way, the way in which, for instance, the worst writing in the world by the worst writers has nevertheless been for many a famous man, especially in politics, the last reading matter of his day, before going to sleep. What was it that Mr. Roosevelt confessed he read every night? Was it *Tarzan*? Or *Riders of the Purple Sage*? Whatever it was, it was trash, but understandably appealing and useful and therapeutic to a mind which all day had been obliged to concentrate sharply upon legal language or diplomatic language, all of it tricky with double and triple meanings and values, and in order to evoke sleep and dreams of a healing nature, sent his soul to the simple pastures of childish fantasy which at least had one very straight simple meaning—for Tarzan to save the white, the pale, English girl, from the sick old tiger, unable to chase and bring down proper running, racing, antelope—and not to save her, not bear in mind to save her from her very lordly, effete, and ineffectual husband. I was very much delighted by the opportunity to run down a long list of names of the most important members of the human family from the beginning of recorded history, and it did not matter that the list had been compiled by one man alone, and nonentity, at that. Who do you have to be to put the great men and women of the human family in a chronological order based upon greatness, which in turn was asked to oblige the human family with influence, whether good or bad. It was a kind of game, and games are always welcome, for as we all know even perfection is soon enough really unbearable, and the reason most sensible men give for not wanting even in fantasy to go to heaven, to perfection, and to be obliged to stay there forever. Such a thought is appalling. It was bad enough in the world, and boredom assailed the soul every day, in spite of all of the easy and really rather lovely distractions, girls for boys, wives for husbands, children, neighbors, colleagues, strangers, adventures, art, literature, and all the rest of it. And so it has always been a compulsion for anybody with a slightly cantankerous nature to shock devout Christians, or others, by rejecting their most profoundly cherished dreams of final and total and ever-lasting fulfillment—in the hereafter, in heaven. I shall not mention the names of those bad boys of journalism and literature whose scoffing I read as a growing boy, but I did consider these daredevils and death-defying boys the real heroes of the world—but after a year or two, long before I was fourteen, for instance, I considered their bravado and belittlement obvious, dull, and even more boring than the mournful longing of great congregations of Presbyterians and Methodists at church singing hymns about the reward ahead—perfection, heaven, and eternity. And along came Jung to offer the suggestion that if multitudes insist that there is a continuation of life after death, this compulsion deserves at least a little looking into, on behalf not of religion but of science. The first name on the list, however, was not Jesus, it was Mohammed, and the reason was very sensible. The Moslem religion was vital to many more people than the Christian religion. What kind of a foetus was Mohammed? Was he a different kind than Jesus? Than you yourself? He must have been, but it is not really something one is able to believe. *1:40 P.M.*

William Saroyan
74 Rue Taitbout 75009
Paris, France
Sunday, July 8, 1979 11:40 A.M.

There is really very little that man needs to know about himself, the magnificent astonishment he must be to anything or anybody. Shall we ask if God or Largeness or Totality is a Person? Good heavens no, that's rather foolish, is it not? Man is quite simply programmed, as the saying is these days of mechanical procedures for attending to the millions of details of human continuation, man is designed to proceed without finding out anything of any real significance about himself, although human poetry suggests that he suspects quite a lot, and what he suspects is full of wonder, love, and even delight, but also with certain of the best poets full of horror, fear, and hatred. The simple fact remains however that man at his most efficient is simultaneously a brillant learner and practicioner of that which permits him to stay alive, and everywhere something very like a simpleton, but a simpleton with eyes that look directly at things or at other persons or animals, at faces, and eyes, and convey by this act of communication something very like wit, comradeship, compassion, and possibly that order of love which certain of us (especially myself, I hope I may say) is both the source and system of all life

62

anywhere—and that is a large order. You do not get living matter from hate. You get dead matter from it. You do not get the compulsion of living matter to begin living matter from hate, it just isn't possible. The reason the life-haters in art, especially painting but more especially in writing, are highly honored appears to be that first the artists have been expert and second that it is desirable for man to hate, even to the point of cessation of belief, of the will to continue, for out of this comes a renewal of all else which we are obliged to think of as love. The fact may very well be that it is not possible, really, for man to hate, for any form of life to hate, and all seeming hatred, all behavior that seems to demonstrate hatred, is tentative, procedural, a symptom of change, of deepening of love, of strengthening of adaptation, as I've heard it, of getting ready for another million years of survival. And a big laugh goes up from the gallery, for there sit the realists, and a million years is far too much for them to think of as a possibility for us, the human branch of life, and most of them have the feeling that with us, in our madness, we shall take all life remaining. Well, we have a situation here so really vast that it is perhaps pointless to speculate about it, although it ought to be clear from anybody, excepting perhaps Lord Russell, who in the last two or three years of his long and raunchy life took to making clear statements about the inevitability now for man to destroy himself—totally. He was thinking about the willful usage of nuclear weapons, and possibly also with what is known as bacteriological warfare. Don't believe it, reader. By all means believe that it is not beyond imagining that nuclear weapons shall be used, and possibly also vast and devastating amounts of deadly bacteria will be released upon ourselves, but even then we shall not succeed in killing off this race. And this is the reason: it can't be done in fact, however totally it is done in theory by the experts. And the speaker is a simpleton, but not with either pride or humility, simply with necessary recognition of the personal reality, which appears to be totally impersonal too, and the property of the whole race. What was Lord Russell like in the womb? He certainly was a slim fellow of great intelligence, industry, superiority (in comparison with specimens far more simple than himself in the few noticeable details), and

in youth a horny fellow, it would seem, and in old age a kind of clean dirty old man. What was he like as a foetus? Did his mother, along with the mother of Mohammed, a far far more influential man, have any sense of what was going on inside her own chemistry, metabolism, and reproductive apparatus? Well, there is no creature which begins which does not feel this one is the one, if it is a single birth-to-be, and if it is a group, then the female surely feels again, not that the litter is to be great, but that one of the four or five or whatever the number may be is surely going to be the one: and dog-breeders seem to be able to go to a newly released litter and pick out the best of the lot and also the least, to give away, or in some cases perhaps to gently destroy, strengthening thereby the line, the breed, and delivering the mother from the added enslavement to feed that one. I think of the survival of Eskimoes in their simple harsh but also complex and loving environment, and I consider these people marvels of intelligence, not rudimentary human forms, for they laugh with their infants.
12:05 P.M

65

William Saroyan
74 Rue Taitbout 75009
Paris, France
Monday, July 9, 1979 11:55 A.M.

What is it in nature, in man, that may be likened to birth, and indeed to pregnancy, to nourishing from one's self something else and somebody else growing inside one's self, so that this entire procedure may perhaps be noticed as being the property, the gift, the curse, as some might put it, of all humanity, female and male alike, and in all nature, and in all living matter? Is there such a likeness, in all truth? There is not, one may be permitted to quickly say, for the enormity of what happens to women who conceive and become pregnant, and wait for the time of deliverance, as it is called, is mysterious, mighty, magnificent, and don't worry, reader, I am not going to ramble along with a lot of words that begin with the letter M, although this is always a temptation that few writers have wanted eagerly to resist. Women conceive, nurture life, contain it within themselves, wait, suffer many kinds of famous illness and forms of hunger, suffer fear (or not, there are many women of many tribes who rather enjoy getting themselves pregnant and then enjoy giving birth even more than they enjoyed the action which got them pregnant, and one such that I have heard about are the women of the Kurdish people, pretty

66

much all of them, for they are walkers by nature and they have the physical health and mental amusement, or joy, about themselves and their men and their kids, and the way of life of all of them, to enjoy the pain of it and the swift-passing pleasure, and also certain Armenian women of certain villages, who according to stories I heard as a small boy, or overheard I should say, women working fields at harvest time, would go to one side with another woman, give birth, bathe the child, feed it, and be back to work within an hour—sometimes the story said that the hoe was replaced by the rifle, the field or farm by rock and river both for cover and escape from the enemy, as in such matters the opposition is called)—suffer fear, or anticipation of plea-sure, at least the anticipation of the pleasure of deliverance, of return to exclusive selfhood, of emptiness, as after a large full movement of the bowels—show me a people whose bowel movements are only partial and I will show you a people given to philosophical speculations, religious dispute, and mistrust of even the father or the brother. Suffer fear, that is to say, or the anticipation of pleasure, deliver themselves of the holy intruder, the secret one, turn him over to the family, to the town, to the world, and all of this is done without any appropriate ritualistic dance or ceremony which would seem to be altogether proper. We are obliged to acknowledge that only women do what only women do: only they give birth to life, connect with something so vast and intricately associated with the total mystery of things and actions, that there is no reason to liken what they do to anything else, especially which men also do. Even so, men are said to experience gestation or the equivalent of it, especially poets, dramatists, novelists, painters, composers, sculptors, bank robbers, assassins, and others whose specific projects require meticulous planning and slow growth. Is there a connection of any kind at all? Well, if one may be permitted to point out something so obvious as the fact that there is nothing disconnected from anything else, slime from flash of luminous thought, for instance, then we can say yes, there is a connection, otherwise there is only a manner of thinking and speaking at work here. A novelist might facetiously or even earnestly remark that he was pregnant with a new novel for the same nine months that his wife was pregnant with their firstborn, and a son, and indeed he was impelled to undertake the writing of that story from the moment that he was informed by his wife that she was pregnant and that in nine months they would behold an heir. This is not however the connection I am thinking of, which I believe has a basis in the kind of reality which is mistakenly said to be scientific and based strictly on provable fact—terms which are absurd at he outset. I am asking if there is something like conception, pregnancy and birth in the human family that is in all life, and while I am unable to reply that there is, and to name it, and demonstrate what I mean, I do believe quite simply that birth itself came as a consequence of the continuance of that action over billions of years, and that the action serves nature and us, members of that branch of life called human, in ways that if ended would deprive us of continuance of surely under a century. *12:20 P.M.*

William Saroyan
74 Rue Taitbout 75009
Paris, France
Tuesday, July 10, 1979 1:55 P.M.

As far as I am able to remember, to know, to imagine, only one birth is celebrated, the birth of Jesus, and this little mystery somehow does not especially trouble me even though I know it should. Was it all invented, then, long after his birth had gone unnoticed? It would seem to have been. In the West, in Europe generally I suppose, and possibly even in Asia, Africa, and other places the anniversary of a birth is celebrated, but if so, if all this is something actual and not presumed, I am obliged to suspect that not everybody wants to celebrate the anniversary of his birth, and that among those who do enjoy such a celebration the fact that the birth is being celebrated seems totally ignored: no reference is made to it at all, nobody is interested, something happened, it happened to the celebrator, he doesn't care why or how, he just likes the celebration. And then of course there have been centuries of people who have come to life and departed from it without any connection with a calendar at all, and have not had any of the details surrounding any birth firmly established. Indeed they haven't really cared. The admonishment that you must be born again suggests that the admonisher had been and the event had meant so much to him he wanted it to be experienced by everybody. How was he born again? Well, we needn't go into the ramifications of a non-physical event, but his birth itself the first time had indeed been physical, even though his mother had not come to pregnancy through her husband, and certainly hadn't found it necessary, possible, or desirable for any reason to inform anybody about having become pregnant by somebody other than her husband, and so what we have is something so sweet and trusting that is has become totally accepted by many people who are not even Christian: she had become pregnant by God, and so she had been informed by an angel, a messenger of God, and so a rather interesting religion or sect of a religion or offshoot of a religion has come into being. His very birth is the highest celebration of that religion, not his birthday, not the party with cake and ice cream, little gifts and candles lighted and blown out. Jews who have looked upon the pregnancy by God with a certain understandable doubt have also nevertheless felt respectful of it, and some Jews have gone through aesthetic or at any rate literary traumas and adventures concerning the validity or falsity theory. When great sensible souls convert to Christianity and are confronted with certain impossibilities they invoke mystery, and they are comforted both by the impossible event itself and by their belief that it is all clear and true in mystery, just as the invention of the universe is, if I may put it that way. In all other areas, however, these converts, or those born into the faith, demand of events a sensible explanation and no mystery at all. No need to belabor faith, and that is what is involved here. Anybody wants to believe something, let him, goes the American expression. Can it harm anybody? No is the implied answer, but the fact is that there has never been a religion, sect, breakaway, or renunciation of a religion that has not harmed somebody, and frequently multitudes. In the name of good, however. Is this itself, then, a renunciation, and is it going to harm somebody? Well, a little perhaps, but not really, and only perhaps a child or childlike person who has found private comfort in a love for Jesus that is a love for self and life and universe and truth and everything else, and the harm is not going to be in that his faith has been exposed as unfounded but that he is sorry to find out that anybody could question his faith, and be such a fool. But the thing that is being chased down here is how did it happen that it was his actual birth that became the big event of his life, legend, art, and mystery, as of course it actually is for everybody, and yet nobody else seems to have noticed the importance of that first event, certainly not in that mighty manner. In folklore births are described that are fanciful falsifications of the real event, but we are all aware that this is to let us know that bragging is part of human nature and that it starts in the belly of the lady who is the mother. Have we overlooked something we ought not to have, and somehow have sought to correct by means of astrological readings, for one thing? It would seem so, and then we must wonder why the human race has pushed ahead and done its business without any real awareness of its start. Why was that? Does it suggest that it takes billions of years for any order of life to be ready for its fullness and its very simple truth? *2:20 P.M.*

William Saroyan
74 Rue Taitbout 75009
Paris, France
Wednesday, July 11, 1979 12:35 P.M.

H. L. Mencken liked to speak up for the Jukes family which had a long history of producing ordinary people who tended to crime, for he loved a paradox, and his argument, although not especially sound, was that if the truth were told about the famous Adams family of Boston we would be astonished and perhaps delighted that essentially they were not much different from the Jukes family. Everybody in each family was born, and nobody and nothing can make the event of birth in the Adams family in any way different or better than it was in the Jukes, and if anything it is likely that the Jukes women took birth in stride, so to put it, and were not especially put out by it, either in love and expectation or in the pain or fear of pain in delivery. All things are shared by all people, and it may very well be that now and then among the Jukes women there were two or three who had more pain and trouble delivering than two or three of the Adams women. The event is universal in all of its procedures, and it varies from climate to climate and culture to culture in only the trappings, and in the expectations or in the sophistications concerning the expectations. The Armenians have an expression, poetic and wise,

74

that does not altogether suit this reality but as it has just come to mind I will see it through and move along: in Armenian the sound is sharp, strong, and mixed of equal parts of scorn and laughter: one beholds a son, a daughter, a group of people, and as they are each at least unattractive and apparently quite stupid, they are referred to as being *ahkh-mahkh gullear-i vahstahk*. This means "idiot cock's crop." Or—well, there is no need to or-it at all. That's what it means and you the reader can put it into other words as you prefer. It is a vulgar expression, used only by men, of men: and for women there may be something else, perhaps a little less cocksure—and if this is a pun, please understand that I do not make puns and am opposed to the making of them, but now and then come upon one, seemingly spontaneous, that delights me. I heard the remark for the first time when I was nine or ten, and the speaker was a young uncle not yet married. He spoke of his cousin and his cousin's two sons and two daughters, all with the coarse features of the father. The children were the crop, and he considered them idiotic, father of the same assortment of boys and girls and apart their father, his cousin, whom he considered contemptible. But a short ten years later he was the father of the same assortment of boys and girls and apart from the fact that his children were brought up as if their father was one of the great men not only of Fresno but of California and indeed, in a way, of the world, and that there was in him a touch of genius, which little by little began to seem to me and to everybody else just a little infected by the same order of idiocy that he had found in his cousin. The point is that a good family seems to assure the parties of good children, and on the whole this is not altogether untrue, and seldom shockingly so, but the fact remains as H. L. Mencken pointed out in *The American Mercury* in the middle 1920s if the Jukes family produces more pickpockets, so to put it, than the Adams family, it also produces more baseball players. And that's nothing to cheer about, there is no such thing. Abraham Lincoln has been referred to endlessly about his famous and probably inaccurately quoted remark about his debt to his mother—not his father. And there will not be another rendering of the remark. There is quite simply no way to dispute the powerful influence of the mother during the child's first four years, and then on through the next ten, even though that influence is supplemented either by that of the father or spread among all men, related or not to the child. It comes to us, it comes to me as not a surprise but a disappointment that so many vital men either had no children at all, or only daughters. Mark Twain would have written the same Huckleberry Finn had he had not one son but three and no daughters, but he also might have written something else, too, out of the absence of the love and sweetness of little girls in the house. Jesus, who claimed that he was the son of God, has not had anybody declaring himself the son of Jesus. A biological connection or a big fat lie, it would still be an exciting piece of information or misinformation for scholarly documentation, as in his own declaration. We can presume, on fair evidence, however, that Mark Twain's son, for instance, might be far more like his mother than like his father. That is the rather exciting truth about the continuation of the race, and surely part of the reason the Rothschilds tended to marry cousins, or other near of kin. *1:00 P.M.*

William Saroyan
74 Rue Taitbout 75009
Paris, France
Thursday, July 12, 1979 11:40 A.M.

What shall I say, my friend, you who were born, my enemy, to take my space, to grab the bread from my hand, to steal my wife, to deprive my son of birth, to deny my daughter her form and face, how shall I let you know, my friend, and you, my enemy, that we are the same, one another, friend, enemy, nothing, nobody, without space, bread, wife, son, daughter, and money, especially money. Nobody unborn is given his portion in money, he gets it, if at all, in the form of, how shall we put it, surely not oblivion, for oblivion implies that he once had something, especially himself. He gets his portion in formlessness which somehow nevertheless edges and pulses toward form, but the hell with all that, reader, let us get down to cases, let us declare straight out that the foregoing was a lark, if indeed it was not a crow, and let us move along to ourselves, reader, and writer, fighting out the hope of a smile, great good God almighty, let us please be granted the message to the brain that compels a smile, for what is a smile if not a rejoicing in the midst of misery? What is a smile if not something like a failure of communication, a vast violent forgetfulness, for God's sake, boy, you're on fire, what are you smiling about? One may not

78

know what one sayeth, as the Scripture perhaps goes, but in whatever one sayeth one may be sure there is absurdity, but putting it into the letters of the prevailing alphabet, and into the words of the prevailing language and usage of it, and into the prevailing sentence structure of the race and place, ah well, then, reader, friend, enemy, stranger, and Lord, Lord, our beloved friend of confusion, we know we are here, do we not? By joining all the others of all times in being breathers, after the nine billion years in the blessed dark of beginning, we know we have been born, we know we are breathing, we know we are here, and we know enough about our absurd connection to everything unknown to understand that it is very probably a good idea to go to lunch. Now, of course one of us is always a little better than another of us, and so who we take to lunch, or who we go to lunch with, as guest, is a matter of great importance, for if we are not careful we shall surely betray our high birth, or on the other hand acknowledge our low birth, the first by going to lunch with an inferior person, the second by being eager to accept the invitation to go to lunch given by a superior person, or at any rate a person we happen to consider superior. It is disgusting, and well it might be, in either event, although if the lunch happens to be superb, we tend to overlook that fact or that unfact, for there is no fact in any area of truth that is not at the same time an unfact, all things are twins, but going to lunch provides us with an excellent opportunity not to care about that at all, and to care very much about the lobsters, at thirty dollars apiece, but cold and altogether lovely. Now doesn't that really make it worthwhile to have been born, to have been bounced out of the saloon where we enjoyed the beer and the free lunch for so long? Most likely not, but it is a thought, it is certainly sensible to consider carefully why so many insufferable people go to so much trouble about going to lunch and getting the best lobsters and all of the best of the rest of the stuff that human beings stuff into themselves endlessly until they leave this new saloon, suffering the humiliation again of being bounced out of the place, and being themselves stuffed into a tiny space in the earth somewhere. What is it that we have to comfort us in the bad weather, to amuse us when entertainment is bankrupt, to buy us toys when money is worthless, to permit us to believe, again, that something is bound to turn up at last that will be the occasion and justification for loud singing and wild dancing, or for the simple sitting and not being at all concerned about anything at all, any movement at all? What is it that we have and can get to if we like and find that we are glad we bothered? Well, reader old brother old sister old father old mother old son old daughter it is the table, it is the level space upon which we set out comestibles, and crockery and silverware and glasses and where we pick up spoon and knife and fork and fall to. Lobsters and oysters, shad and roe, caviar and sole, ah, glory glory, isn't it preposterous that we eat these innocent beautiful brothers and sisters as if they were not persons, as if they were only things? But if not such marvels of design and structure, how about if we eat only a piece of bread with a good round onion, and wash it down not with wine but with tap water, will that also do? Bet your ass it will, sir. *12 NOON*

81

William Saroyan
74 Rue Taitbout 75009
Paris, France
Friday, July 13, 1979 11:25 A.M.

A great man is a great man, is he not? But what was he at birth? He very nearly didn't get started, and then after he had burst into breathing and crying at once, it was touch and go whether he would go on breathing or stop for a good long time, was it not? Well, it's really none of our business, of course, for the simple fact of the matter is and always has been not how close he came to not being, but being itself, and if there is a boy around about, or a girl, that is what we see and know and accept. Somebody is there, and we forget (if we ever knew) how his chances were very poor and then suddenly he was past all interference and on his way, although there was never a day or a night, an hour or a moment, during which he might not come to his end, for accidents happen, like the accident of birth itself, the accident of this man and this woman embracing, the accident of their essences embracing, the accident out of millions of chances that the consequence turned out to be this boy: Julius Caesar, born 100 B.C., for instance, and for instance. Well, was he a great man? And the answer is it is not necessary for him to have been a great man, or for you to be a great man, reader, or for anybody anywhere now or

82

then, long ago or coming up in the next century, to be a great man. Nobody is great, nobody is greater than anybody else, for the reason that everybody is everybody else, and something unplanned and unforeseen. It is impossible for any man to be greater than the race, but now and then when somebody turns out to have an appearance of greatness by act or utterance or by any measure of any kind it is convenient for everybody to consider that he was great, he is great, and I look around to see of whom that might be said right now, and I find that it cannot be said of anybody and also that it must be said of anybody, another big fat and damned boring contradiction, and piece of bad writing, but let me tell you this, reader, I don't have to write only good writing, it is permissible for me, and indeed it is desirable for me to do a good amount of bad writing, and if you were to ask why this is so, do you know at this moment I am not prepared to say, although I know that I am not mistaken in what I have put forward as the truth, or certainly not greatly mistaken. Julius old buddy was born on this very day a good one hundred years before Jesus was born, and in human terms that is a fair piece of time gone, and a good long time after Julius was murdered by the mob, his own mob, Shakespeare wrote a play about it, and this is something that was performed in part, in very small part, by certain pets of certain teachers at Longfellow Junior High in Fresno in 1919, and hundreds of thousands of similar productions of Shakespeare's *Julius Caesar* have been performed all over the world every year endlessly. Why? Is it because Julius was great, or is it because William was great, or is it because there is a terrible desperation in the human heart that is somewhat eased by performing parts of other people in other pieces of reality, or fantasy, or by witnessing such performances. Well, again take your pick, it doesn't matter, it all settles down again to being a little part of the human story, and the longer we survive the larger and more complicated that story becomes in its daily events and the more difficult it becomes to tell even one tiny smidgen of it in a way that can possibly be of any use to anybody, and is totally ignored by the human race itself, as of course we all know even the works of the greatest playwright of all time are ignored. He was a Roman, Julius was, he was an Italian if you will, he was high born, as the saying is, he went in for

84

learning and cultivated behavior and speech, and he got himself seduced into politics, and that cost him his life, although Anthony in his famous speech written for him by Shakespeare hundreds of years after Anthony was dead and buried, Anthony said some rather nice things about his friend Caesar and some sarcastic things about Brutus, very rhythmic and much more justified than the rhythmic experiments of such contemporary writers as Gertrude Stein, or a couple of dozen much more recent hop heads who go in for all kinds of tricks of writing, like making collages of torn pages from books of all kinds and presenting the hodgepodge as not only their own but as profundities about the meaninglessness of something or somebody. Well, Anthony seemed to have been sensibly eloquent with the help of Shakespeare, and in the Longfellow Junior High production of about half an hour of the great play a sissified boy performing Anthony looked and sounded precisely the same as he did in class and playground—sissified and silly, and where are they now? These heroes of Rome and stage and school? Everywhere, folks, the same as ever, the busy little bastards are charging around everywhere. *11:55 A.M.*

William Saroyan
74 Rue Taitbout 75009
Paris, France
Saturday, July 14, 1979 12:05 P.M.

When I think how easy it is to be alive, how really endurable it is not to be something else (other than alive), how simple it is to get one from one minute to the next and so from one day to its night, and from one night to its morning, and all the rest of it, carrying the soul from birth to death, whatever those words may really mean, if we could somehow see to it, and when I remember how much grumbling and growling every man seems to need to do just to maintain something like willingness to go on, and how much crying and carrying-on every woman seems obliged to do to be, each of them, her own dear self, or her own terrible self. At those moments of diminished willingness, or fullness of character, and when I notice how so much of everything everywhere that has life whether animal or plant, or motion as a river flows and an ocean sends a wave in and receives the same spent wave back, by a law of moon and mystery, and when I remember the desperation that drove me to unbelievably boring and empty years of petty gambling, I say to myself, Hoo Boy, hoo Man, why have you been such a fool, how does it happen that you have been so blind, so deaf, so numb in the soul as not to have seized every moment's miracle and mightiness and put it to sensible use? And even while I ask the question I begin to feel, to suspect, and finally to know that it is ridiculous, it is absurd, it is silly, it is a fool's question, and yet somehow all those years of youth spent far from the university, spent down on the street of drifters, failures, bums, all trying to come upon redeeming grace by making winning bets on horse races, or at the dumbest card game ever invented to beguile a wasted man's wasted soul and permit him to believe he is still in the game, still a great player waiting for his chance to prove it, he is still himself, the fellow who was born that time, out of the pain and pleasure of the mother, and with expectations in her heart and in the heart of the universe, possibly dead center of the sun itself, that he would indeed be the one, and do his glorious stuff, not only to permit her to take pride in the kind of woman she was when she permitted his father's seed to fall upon and seize her egg and between the seed an the egg to arrange with eternity and truth to start this incredible infant, boy, lad, youth, and man—his name and fame known down the boulevards and streets of the whole living world, and then on and on into the worlds of the future—Grossbiermanoff you say, Gustave von Grossbiermanoff you say, that great one of the world, that's who he is, he was, walking down Third Street in San Francisco in 1929 as if he were nothing more than a bum, just another bum, a petty gambler at rummy, for Christ's sake, sitting hour after hour arranging a new hand of ten idiotic cards, and hoping that this time he will indeed get two triples and one four-card spread and thereby win twenty-five cents, but in the coin of that realm, at Breen's, at the Kentucky, at the Barrell House, which coin was broken down to an exchange value of six for a quarter in cash, or five for a quarter in purchasing power at the bar and at the cigar and cigarette counter, or at the restaurant: it was madness, that's what it was, leaving the glory of the sunlight out at the beach, out where the Pacific comes past Seal Rocks and all along the miles of rough sand and hard pebbles entirely without the charm of pebbles on other beaches, it was stupid being Gustav von Grossbiermanoff, partly Russian, you know, but also on the maternal side with a fascinating little woman from Asiatic Siberia who received the seed of that forefather who had been somewhat adopted by Poushkine himself, and who knows what other glories ran in his lineage, in his geneaology, only to windup as the bum of Third Street, aged suddenly sixty-six and coughing from cigarettes and willing to bother his head about the stupid cards involved in rummy, and not to go back to his truth and let the whole world know his full and true identity. Think of it, for several great years I looked at hundreds of such faces as that of Gustav von himself and saw nothing but a straight simple boring bum. And so I tried to break free of that dismal usage of precious time by getting a job or being accepted at the University of California, without proper required credits as a high school graduate, and didn't get a job, and was turned away by the Registrar at the University. Do I hold the world responsible for my failure to become who I really am? Of course I do, and so do you, dear reader—they kept you back, the dirty sons of bitches, you know they did. *12:30 P.M.*

William Saroyan
74 Rue Taitbout 75009
Paris, France
Sunday, July 15, 1979 12:10 P.M.

Who would you rather been born? Jesus, Grock, or yourself? Well, the question is another of those Beautiful Silly
Fun Questions and while there are many people who
straight from first breath to last breath believe they were
cheated when they were born themselves, they were the
victims of terrible discrimination, they were the victims of a
dirty trick, most people, most males, most females, do settle
quite early for the proposition that not only are they
themselves, they agree that it is probably not a kind of
arrogance to be glad to be themselves. Nature does that, of
course and indeed nature does everything and we permit
ourselves the great solace of imagining that our thinking,
our imagining, our inventing, our making comes from
ourselves, and not from nature, but the chances that this is
actually so are very slim. We are a part of nature from the
word go. Go. The word. Has been said. And nature said it,
although in this instance it would appear to be that I said it,
you said it, reader, we said it, man said it, but it just is not so,
nature said it, nature permitted us to say it, nature
commanded that we say it, and so it has been with all our
art, science, religion, philosophy, and that damned list gets

more boring everytime we are willing to think of it. Nobody and nothing did it excepting the one vastness which is nature, things, actions, beyond ken, beyond knowing, so that whenever we make a slight half-successful foray into the dark dimension of the unknown, as when Mr. Einstein justified his clumsiness and terrible skill at the violin by hitting up the formula that has come to us in the form of nuclear fission which in turn has been seized by paranoid governments and executed in the form of high explosives for warfare or the threat of it in the old game which we have always used as the occasion to notice the incurable folly of the human race when indeed it has been nature again all the time, when Mr. Einstein, Alfred if that is his first name; hit upon that tiny discovery all of us imagined that we were now approaching full knowledge and that mystery was about to be the victim of light and understanding. Nobody (other than perhaps Mr. Einstein himself) was prepared to consider this foray anything more than the spectacular and theatrical and astonishing little foray that it really was, everybody was willing to believe that man had again scored a tremendous breakthrough (I was about to say breakfast) into the domain of God, as we invented God to serve the purpose of covering up our feeble ability to grasp largeness and complexity and unity beyond ourselves, perhaps our skulls, egg-shaped, and neatly limited and limiting. Jesus, yes, but who's this Grock, and why would anybody ask anybody if instead of having been born himself might he have wanted to be Grock? Well, Grock was this famous clown, according to the legend, who made people laugh so heartily that they forgot anything but that odd hysterical spurious joy (and watch it folks I am a laugher, and I say what I say with thought, even though I love to laugh and value laughter very nearly above even knowledge or wisdom or intelligence, above everything perhaps excepting grace, which is beyond any formula or ability to understand, and the Entirety is endowed with grace however also endowed it is with violence, fire, storm, disintegration, bad taste, cruelty, pain, and death). I see an excuse to laugh in all things, including arithmetic as employed in financial reports, prayers, eulogies (especially for monsters but even more especially for saints), and everything else that is nameable, and the reason is that the unnameable to me compels hilarious laughter. Well, Grock would go out every night in his clown's costume and mask and very nearly kill everybody with the laughter he compelled in them. Oh, I nearly died laughing, everybody said to everybody. And then one evening across from the Circus at a table in a dismal little dive sat a small dull man sipping a cup of tea, or a beer, or a glass of wine, and sobbing softly and shamelessly. When he was asked by somebody if there was anything to be done for him, to end his sorrow, he replied no, there was not. The touched spectator of this pathetic example of inconsolable sorrow went to the manager, owner, bartender and said he would like to know who the little crying man might be. And of course, as you knew all the time, it was Grock. So wouldn't you like to have been Grock instead of who you were at birth? (Do you like that question? It is hilarious to me. It doesn't mean anything at all, how could I possibly not find it hilarious—for everything we have that we take such pride in is like that.) *12:35 P.M.*

William Saroyan
74 Rue Taitbout 75009
Paris, France
Monday, July 16, 1979 12:20 P.M.

Imagine if you will this piece of small drama somewhere
sometime during the brief course of our visitation on earth.
The man says, "Who is it?" The woman says, "I don't know."
"Well, look will you please and let me know, and right now,
not tomorrow." "All right, all right, we are all busy here
with our work on these occasions, so yes, here he is, here he
is, he is you, sir, there are his things." "I don't mean me,
woman, I mean who is he, I know the kind he is, my kind, my
father's kind, his father's kind, but is this one perhaps the
great Hoogli Hoosayn?" "Well, man, I really wouldn't know
about that, give the poor boy a moment to catch his breath
before you ask of him if he is perhaps the great, who, who
did you say, man?" "Hoogli Hoosayn, I said, and I say it
again, the great Tartar warrior, the ravager of peoples and
places." "But, man, have you forgotten, we are not Tartars,
whoever they are, we are one of the many peoples ravaged
by them one of the many places, Middle Mutuff, so why do
you ask is this raging man here, what's his terrible name
again?" "Hoogli Hoosayn, and there is no sense in continuing this talk with you, woman, you are inferior, you are
able to do only woman's work, tilling the soil, fetching the

94

water, preparing the comestibles, and everlasting swelling the belly with some mysterious ailment which turns out to be another of these, and each of them clearly nobody of any consequence, and if I had any gumption at all believe you me kiddo I would hopscotch away from this cave and join the assassins of Hoogli Hoosayn, but there we are, woman, there we are, I've grown accustomed to your face." "You're staying, then, are you? Because if you are please go out and catch a chicken for a good feast of the soup of the chicken and a little pearl barley added." Imagine old friend if you will the whole thing all over again, for the devil of it: Who is it? It is yourself. Again? Well, last time it was myself, so it is only right, that one for me, one for you, is to be the way it goes. How many of us do we have so far? Four of me and four of you, shall we then have more? Well most likely but not this minute, if you don't mind. Is that the only thing you think about—your pleasure? Nothing about what is the stars? What is the moon? Someday somebody on an island somewhere is going to ask those two basic questions, and everybody is going to sit up and take notice, and we are all of us going to learn to cut down a little on the small talk and get out into the big talk—for we have got to if we are not to remain small forever. Well, then, since you asked the questions, please answer them, also. We're not going anywhere and you have informed me that there is nothing better to do than bandy words about instead of you know what. "Tell me, sir, tell me, please, what is the stars? What is the moon?" "I'll tell you, woman, I'll tell you. See this clenched fist, see this open hand, see my face turned purple with you know what if you are going to start you-know-what-ing-me, the stars is those sparklers in the sky, and the moon is the father of them." "The father, man? Really, I thought the moon must very probably be the mother, for she has the roundness of every woman's you know what, and you just don't have the roundness I have, you see, although some men do, and possibly one of you among the four, also a higher pitched voice, and less hair, will you talk to Percival one day soon, man to man, tell him before it is too late that he is one of you, not one of me, man, unless you want him to confuse us all." "Just shut your mouth, woman, just shut it, all of me is me, and the stars is the stars, and the moon is the moon, and his name shall be Hawk, for I have always deeply admired that moose." "The Hawk is not a moose, man, you have got to systemise your knowledge, or we shall never know our you know whats from our you know wheres." "Shut the mouth please, woman, just shut it, it is not fitting that every time you get this mysterious illness and then put out another of them that come out that way, you find fault with my apparatus of gathering, I am as good a gatherer as ever gathered, and whether it is a bantyhen for soup with pearl barley or new information about what to do with a round rock about the size of a ripe eggplant, I am the gatherer, you are at best the gatheree." "Well, man, I suppose I am, at that, there is something along the lines of what you say that might be considered valid, but tell me, sire, please tell me what it is that you feel might be done with a round rock, pray tell." " It is so revolutionary, I hesitate to tell even you, my gatheree, but it came to me like a revelation—bash the rock upon the head of the enemy." *12:50 P.M.*

William Saroyan
74 Rue Taitbout 75009
Paris, France
Tuesday, July 17, 1979 12:55 P.M.

Are you willing to entertain an idea, to consider a kind of theory, to suspect that it is not something new, that it is not in any sense out of order, and that it might just be amusing to God and possibly even to Nature, and very definitely to the Human Race, one part of it raging against, the other in favor of it. Wombs for Hire, so to put it. An established geneaologically sound and even special female specimen, in excellent health, hires out to conceive anybody's continuance in the form of a male or a female, receives the cash upon conception, or at any rate half of it, and the balance upon delivery, whereupon the transaction is concluded, the male goes off with his prize, to take to his sterile or inferior wife, let's say, or to some other woman, and I need not name who they might be, they would tend to be female, that's all, although it is understandable that in these days it could be a male with strong female aspirations, and the newborn infant would be placed in waddling clothes, and fed at the breast or out of a bottle in accordance with preferences, and the male or father would slowly, very slowly begin to observe what he had got out of the transaction: had he got himself the grand bargain he had surely believed he was

98

bound to get because the woman was of a superior line, so that whatever his own line might be his offspring, his child, his heir, the carrier of his seed and name, would have at least half a chance and half a lineage worthy of being put into that loaded word, for if the truth is told there is not lineage that is not as worthy as any other, most likely? Each is certainly within the bounds of human continuity and if mainly slobs have come from this particular line, there have also been saints and soloists with the St. Louis Symphony Orchestra, as I once actually heard it put by a drunken young lady who had miscarried and after three months was still troubled by who the little bastard might have turned out to be, for she had no idea which of the seven or eight lovers may have been the father. Now, this speculation, this proposition, this notion, that good strong women with excellent talent for conception, gestation, parturition, and disappearance, may indeed have been established in not one but perhaps several fairly evolved and sophisticated socie-ties, and I stand only out of reach of this information by some kind of accident. And if there has not been such a general procedure, there have been many women, who independently, in business for themselves, so to put it, have engaged in such dealings, with signed affidavits or contracts, and with very probably not entirely undesirable or unfortunate consequences, which have happened readily in the comparatively traditional arrangements between families and members of them taken to the block in marriage, as it might be put, or danced in joy about the pretty prospect of the future. You can scarcely open an issue of a newspaper in which some piece of actual legal or illegal information concerning the consequences of such a transaction are set before the world, and sometimes there is even a photograph of the woman, suing the man for the return of her beloved son, because she claims she sold him in ignorance and desperation and did not know he was going to turn out to be the marvel he did turn out to be in a matter of a mere eleven years—defeating at chess the greatest players, and saying that all that he was and all that he would ever be he owed to his father who made him, actually forced him, to study chess from even before he could speak, and so on and so forth. Leasing the womb is nothing new, in short, and if the truth is told it is unavoidable, even in the very best of marriages, in which also, horror of horrors, there is an inescapable element of whoring on the part of the ladies and of pimping on the part of the gentlemen. Surely we have all read stories in which, not especially subtly, a junior officer finding his superior glancing at the junior officer's luscious wife speaks to the older man in discreet words which actually come to an open invitation to have her, sir, I will not make a scene or protest, and I mean ever. I believe it was in a Guy de Maupassant short story that I first chanced upon this event, and although I was only a very young man of eleven or twelve, and I found the behavior of the young officer really shabby, I was not shocked, for it seemed to me that there could be extenuating circumstances on both sides, on all three sides indeed, that even the writer did not know about, could not suspect, or deliberately chose to neglect. "Wombs for hire" is not all that strange, in short, and on the other side there is no doubt that neither is "cocks for hire." *1:15 P.M.*

William Saroyan
74 Rue Taitbout 75009
Paris, France
Wednesday, July 18, 1979 12:05 P.M.

On this day in 1811 in Calcutta was born himself, William Makepeace Thackeray, who wrote and published just about at the same time that Charles Dickens did, and of course Charley Boy stole all the glory and profits, while Willie Boy watched with something like envy and annoyance, for in his own way Mr. Thackeray was very good, and he went to America, as Charlie Boy did several times, and gave talks on the English Comic Writers or some such, including that cranky and really mean loner Jonathan Swift. but this won't do, either, for it is birth that I am brooding about, specifically birth inside the animal family which is designated the human, and how and why it started and appears never to be ready to stop, and of course there is the expectation in my heart that without research and study and the usage of language remote from ordinary word-language, as in Latin and Armenian and English, without scientific and mathematical and other languages, it is the expectation, without undue hope and therefore also without undue disappointment in the event of failure, total failure, it is nevertheless the easy loping expectation that perhaps by the Grace of God, the same as all of us love and

102

some of us hate and a few wish to approach, in grace, as Kirkor Narekatsi, the berserk ecclesiastic of Ancient Armenia, or ancient enough, although in all truth he lived and wrote quite recently as far as my understanding of time in all of its dimensions goes. Inshallah, if God grants it, perhaps I will be standing at my work table thinking about the birth of Willie Thackeray in 1811 which was precisely one hundred and three years before my birth in 1908, no connection of course, excepting actually that the connection is so close it is impossible to make any sense of it, and as I thinking about Mr. Thackeray talking to the ladies of Boston and New York and Chicago, and sometimes to their husbands, and to their growing daughters and perhaps even their small sons, I may just suddenly half unknowingly say something about human birth that has always been true but not said, and we shall have the benefit of that small piece of added something or other, for it has been my experience from the beginning that if a writer will stand and confront the enemy, the ally, the would-be assassin, the good Samaritan, it will follow that something quite good instead of something rotten may come of it, and it has always given

103

me the most remarkable kind of mixture of pleasure and astonishment when I myself have been the messenger involved: I have been the writer of the words, and the next day, like Charles Dickens himself, I have been the reader of the words, as if I had not written them in the first place, as if they were written by themselves, or by God, or by Nature, as I had earliest believed that all books were, events of nature like new grass and trees. Getting to know what I wrote last night was something especially appealing to me when my working hours were sometime after perhaps eight o'clock at night and sometime before four in the morning, for in those days of youth, or comparative youth, writing with intense concentration at night, smoking one Chesterfield unfiltered regular cigarette after another and drinking one cup of coffee after another, the spirit straining after everything but also very much at ease about everything almost invariably soon arrived at the place where it is all located, for all of us, for the whole human race, the place where the Metenataran, as the Armenians put it, is located, the place of the ancient manuscripts, the library of all time, and the place of all experience not just to my own few ancestors but to all of our ancestors, and the place of meeting, of discussion, of decision, and the place of prayer, homage to ourselves, the place of learning, the place of song and dance, so that being at work at my own writing from that place, all of them gathered together into the one place of the race gone but still here in myself, I wrote things of which I knew not as the saying might be, and then the next day, after sleeping a sleep that was a continuation of attendance at that place, at that school, at that social hall, I was delighted and astonished by what I had written. It could happen again, I am saying. In Calcutta in the compound where the Armenian Church and School was located, I was taken by a priest and shown a plaque which said that William Makepeace Thackeray was born in that room, and the room was being carefully and sweetly preserved and restored in smooth white plaster, and standing there with the Priest I said to myself, By God, this is great, the Armenians have come into the ownership of the room in which a fine writer was born, and I remembered Rouben Mamoulian directing a movie of *Vanity Fair* called *Becky Sharp*, with Miriam Hopkins. *12:25 P.M.*

William Saroyan
74 Rue Taitbout 75009
Paris, France
Thursday, July 19, 1979 12:50 P.M.

If you're going to earn your day's leisure, like your day's bread, you had better see to it, but who earns his birth, one may perhaps be permitted to ask, or even who earns his death, for the boys put down in wars go to unearned deaths, and who is it among your acquaintances, friends, or family lives a life so fully itself that his death must also be understood to be fully itself, his own, and not Nature's. Or so I stand and put forward, for it is my work especially at this time in this work to speculate and speculate about all things starting with birth, and with the emphasis there pretty much throughout, insofar as that might be possible for me, or indeed for any of us, for it isn't that the mind wanders, it is only that itself is made out of wanderings, at birth, at conception, and these wanderings are so vast and varied and all-pervading, as I believe the word is, that there is no possibility of catching up and processing it all, and at the second birth, by which I mean death of course, we shall have only added to the original wanderings by the smidgen of them that are our own, these days enlarged, considered in a exterior sense, by aviation, and diminished considerably in an interior sense by drugs and alcohol and fucking, or

106

fucking around, sometimes called womanising, as in the case of the one-eyed lad of Israel, somebody wrote some-where, Moishe Dayan, daughter a novelist, son a film actor, and in reading that information one felt, Ah, no, neither is it necessary to report this, nor to put it that way, but whatever it may be has to be put some way, and after drugs and alcohol and poontang, as poor Thomas Wolfe dead all these years since 1938 put it, our own individual tribal regional wanderings are simultaneously increased and diminished, so that whatever it may be said (to ourselves, or to God) that we have added to the original wanderings which came in the package of birth itself, it is cluttered and really impossible to know any more than one knows the vast wanderings already there inside each of us on arrival. I love the famous American novels (I know of no such Russian, German, French, Italian novels, but perhaps there are some in English writing, and for that matter in all writing, we must presume that this is more likely than not) in which the novelist, taking the role of the teller of a tale, the narrator, or the persona, as literary writers took to calling it about thirty years ago, starts the saga by saying,

My father told me two things that I have remembered and found both useful and useless so far: in public behave with all women as if they are virgins, in private as if they are whores. And he is off to the races, is he not. Well, go on, go on, what was the second thing? Well, in the popular novels it was always something about drinking or gambling or making friends or making enemies, and then like as not the novelist, doing his first and most famous novel, might go on to say, and then he surprised me by reversing himself entirely, saying, In public behave with all women as if they are whores, but in private as if they are virgins. Who are these fathers with the wisecracks? Well, they are ourselves, the readers, and now and then, as in this instance, the writer, and in 1874 when my father Armenak was born, in Bitlis, in the Armenian highlands, also the Kurdish highlands, but also claimed by the government as Turkey and considered the Turkish highlands, his father being Betros or Peter and his mother being Hripsime, after the sweet saintly girl from Rome, who was martyred by the very king who wanted to have her in his bed, and she wouldn't leave the bed of Jesus, what did my father know in all of his interior wanderings that I may imagine that if the time ever came for him to tell me something to remember throughout my own life, what would it be? Well, it could be just about anything out of his character certainly up to his thirty-sixth year when he died, and perhaps for all I know in one of his most profound spells of melancholy, also called neurasthenia, also called depression, and finding me nearby did indeed address a few remarks to me, uncomprehending as I was, and certainly unequal to keeping inside my soul forever the burden of wisdom in his remarks: My son, don't be a Christian fool like your father, but also don't be a Pagan fool like the ancient Armenians, your father's ancestors and therefore also your own, see if you can somehow work it that you will be a fool in your own way, with your own reasons, excuses, and meanings. Thank you, Father, I can imagine myself saying in reply, and then forgetting the whole silly business. *1:10 P.M.*

William Saroyan
74 Rue Taitbout 75009
Paris, France
Friday, July 20, 1979 12:50 P.M.

My problem is that in this work of writing I am waiting for the arrival of a procedural system that will make the writing inevitable, unavoidable, and even appealing every morning first thing in the day, and this arrival goes right on just failing to happen, so that every day I am obliged to be Born Again, so to put it, and as Jesus said and we all learned at Sunday School or from our Christian friends who learned at Sunday School that you must be born again. Well, I'm willing, always have been, getting born again is one of the unexperienced events I am not opposed to keeping an open mind about, as I am opposed to about many other possible events, including (as Aldous Huxley seemed to believe did him much good) the taking of various kinds of drugs. Air and water and self are drugs enough for me, so that when my son long ago, smoking a joint, urged me to smoke one also, I had to refuse, remarking that I didn't want either the peace of it, or the stimulation, and in any case I had given up smoking. Well, what is the procedural system that I am hoping for? It is quite simply this: an easy guide for the continuation of daily writing on the subject of birth. Is that too much to ask? It appears to be, so far, but I do still

110

entertain hopes of having the reward of patience, even while I go on writing and writing without benefit of any kind of procedural system other than my determination, and my opinion, which is surely stupid, that anything I write is interesting, and I mean to you, and you, and you, as Walter Winchell used to scream on the radio forty or more years ago every Sunday night, Mr. and Mrs. America. But I go even further and say, Also to you, Mr. and Mrs. England, France, Germany, Italy, Spain, Russia, China, Japan, and the hell with it, enough is enough. The *New Yorker* magazine in some connection or another once noticed that several of my books as catalogued at the Public Library on Fifth Avenue, a famous place in my experience, especially during my first visit to New York, in 1928, especially in the snow out front on the steps, beside the lions of stone, as snow fell just after Christmas of that year and just before New Year's Eve, when all of a sudden as the sweet snow fell, my very soul all but fainted with the sweetness of mortality, especially after about ten days of dismal fighting off a bad case of influenza, alone in a tiny room rented from the maiden Halperin sisters, small and intellectual, who taught something or other, perhaps music, somewhere—and in the story or fragment up front in the *New Yorker* the anonymous reporter said that after the printed word on the catalog card for one of my books, after the word Subject, had been typed the word None. This delighted my restored soul (after the episode in the snow) for it seemed to me that again the specialists in books had demonstrated their ineptitude, for we know that it is impossible for a book not to have a subject, and what the trained librarian meant by none was quite simply that the subject was not within the range of the preferences of librarians. The subject was myself, was self, was literature, was writing, was the reader, was experience, was death, and as it is right now in this book is birth, and the procedural system that I employed in the writing of a book about dying, about death, was while useful in getting the book written called *Obituaries*, not very much more meaningful than that, which is useful enough: I took the Necrology list published in *Variety* for the year just gone, which had been the year 1976, and name by name, alphabetically, I daily for perhaps forty-four days or possibly eighty-eight, I don't remember, used each name to turn my

112

writing loose about both the name, the person to whom it had been attached, who was now dead, about his life and career and meaning insofar as I had heard about them, and about himself, as I knew him, for one in ten or twenty of the names belonged to people I had met and had seen with my own eyes and had spoken with, and had listened to as they spoke with me, and with others. That is part of what I mean by a procedural system, something that in Hollywood and on Madison Avenue would be referred to as a gimmick, an embarrassing fact to acknowledge, but if something works, and that procedural system did work, it really doesn't matter if it is called a gimmick, or indeed if it is actually so, the thing that matters is the writing that has come out of the employment of the procedure, and I may say, reader old pal, that even this, which does mater, does not matter all that much. You can live without it without any difficulty at all, but you cannot live without yourself and the purpose of this kind of writing is to beguile you into finding yourself.
1:10 P.M.

William Saroyan
74 Rue Taitbout 75009
Paris, France
Saturday, July 21, 1979 11:55 A.M.

Sam Bass, 1851; Frances P. Keyes, 1885; Ernest Hemingway, 1899; Marshall McLuhan, 1911; Issac Stern, 1920: these four men and this woman Frances were born on July twenty-first of the various years mentioned, but now the year is 1979, and at least a few of the born people have become the unborn or the dead people, certainly Sam Bass about whom I know nothing at all. And of course there were thousands of other people born on July twenty-first, which today happens to be a Saturday in Paris, where I stand at my easel work-table, to do my day's work, a fair piece of new written stuff will come to pass as a consequence, and it is the placing of the present tense into the past tense which is the mark of the professional writer and of any civilization as we of the West understand the matter. We are planners, we look ahead, we predict, we anticipate, and we take into account the inevitability of various things including morning, noon and night, as the famous overture or waltz goes, and the seasons, and in ourselves change, and we like to try to imagine that we shall see to it, shall have seen to it that the change shall be for the better. And we have seldom been mistaken, although when we have been mistaken we have

114

been violently mistaken, as in our little failures to grow up, as in wars, and we are devoted to the proposition that this refusal to grow up is proper for us, and that what we have got to do is insist on our various differences to the point of scratching each other's eyes out like whores in a house where business has been bad and somebody believes somebody else has behaved improperly and to this one must not roar out hah hah hah or har har har, one must simply move along to the truth or seeming truth about the hysterical anxiety and suspicion and fear of America and Russia and China and Japan and France and England and Germany and Israel and Egypt and India and all of the other countries, one for the other, even while the ladies begin to suspect that the gentlemen of their beds are not really gentlemen, but are husbands and lovers and fathers of the infants that the ladies put forth and out of womb into world in proper season. But if it isn't all right, and something to take lightly or even with comic derision, it is also not all that bad, rotten, criminal, imbecilic, either. Or so we say. The names I have mentioned I have come upon in a kind of non-book or trick-book entitled *1975 Birthday and Horoscope*

Engagement Calendar With Your Daily Forecast, which was sent to me that year, or late in 1974, by the publisher, because I am in the book, I am listed in it like one of the immortals. The book is compiled by Erika and William Glover and a copy is inscribed to me "For William Saroyan with warmest wishes for many happy birthdays yet to come Sincerely Wm Glover" and I have made a note and a drawing in red on the inside thick cover dated Paris Wednesday August 31 1974 4 PM from *IHT* (*International Herald Tribune*). Apparently the thing was sent to me in care of the greatest little paper in the English language in the world, and they in turn forwarded it to me. I remember away back in 1959, twenty years ago, standing out front of that place when it was on Rue de Berri chatting with an editor who had been with the *Paris Herald* and in Paris at the time when the American Lost Generation had been in town, but that man has since died and I somehow am not sure of his name, although sometimes I am sure of it, and of course he did not suspect that his fond recollections of those times and those people (who were

116

anything but) were boring me because I am polite and because I can indeed find even the boring quite fascinating, for let us remember that I was born, and that seems to be one of the conditions of birth but not one of the best or greatest of them—make anything that comes along useful to you somehow, and you will find boredom quite entertaining. And of course the gentle soul who was about sixty to my fifty at the time, out front at Twenty-one Rue de Berri, the gentle man, who also wrote editorials for the paper, had great warmth for the gone days and souls, and even though Ernest Hemingway was still alive at the time, and had two years to go, the man spoke of him as if he were already dead, because in the old days he was arriving, he was young, he was coming into the fullness of his talent, he was getting set to write *The Sun Also Rises*—but now what? The poor man was sixty years old and not very happy about anything or anybody, and Hemingway became the *Paris Herald* editorial writer, and vice versa, and do you know what? It was not boring, actually. *12:25 P.M.*

117

William Saroyan
74 Rue Taitbout 75009
Paris, France
Sunday, July 22, 1979 11:55 A.M.

I have forgotten more than you will ever know—that is one of the remarks of small boys in disputes about comparative intelligence, but I am saying to myself that I have indeed forgotten more than I have written, ever, and right now I keep forgetting more than I should, or certainly more than is good for me, more than is right for this work. Ah, well, it happens, and it happens, and it happens, and who are we, who am I, to be especially annoyed that it does. Everything happens, and forgetting how to write is one of them for a writer. Who gets born, isn't that the question? And the answer is, the sons of bitches get born, and the saints who are trained by the family and the world to forget it, and usually do, although now and then one or another of them is unable to forget it. You get born, and I get born, and a good thing, too, and I'll tell you why. It seems to be more interesting to have been born than not to, although even I in a moment of absurdity have remarked that perhaps the greatest achievement is for anybody not to get born. What nonsense, what astonishing stupid nonsense, but let it go, forget it, saint, make nothing of it, son of a bitch, move along and know that moving is the idea, and be glad you can,

118

for that is part of the procedure that follows the event of having been born, and man it was a long time ago for me, although hardly as long ago for me as it was long ago for a friend who writes poems but has earned his living as a lawyer, specialising in libel, especially in books, Melville Cane, who was born one hundred years ago, or at any rate three or four months ago celebrated in New York his one hundredth anniversary, but I couldn't go, so I wrote to him, and he replied, You can make a hundred, too—just take good care of yourself, and I believe he went on to say, be self-centered, eat sensibly, drink very sensibly, and so it went. But I keep forgetting, even now, the things I was sure would come to me from the storehouse and make this work the thing it ought to be, which I believe it will still become, even if I go right on forgetting. Well, how could that be? Well, it could be from the balance which is in all action: if you forget, then to balance it, if you remember, even if it is something irrelevant, it follows that something out of this will balance the forgetting, and something else will balance something else, and high blood pressure will settle back down, and the heart will relax, and the head will not flood with blood and confusion, and the ears will not take off in a concert of ringing that make the musical forays of John Cage seem juvenile by comparison, and the head swims, and the balance fails, or would, or would, except that you have been born and you have found out how to manage your good fortune in that fact and in that fantasy. What I mean is, I am not forgetting right now that while it is time to do my day's work on this book, I am actually in poor shape for it, almost in impossible shape for it, and the Concerto for Ringing Ears informs me boy it is time to lay off, that's all. But I will notice that on July twenty-second, this very day in Paris, Rose Kennedy was born in 1890, Karl Menninger in 1893, Alexander Calder in 1898, (ten years before my birth, and I was boarding a transatlantic airplane at Charles de Gaulle airport when I saw the headline Alexander Calder is dead and that was only two years or so ago), Amy Vanderbilt in 1908 (my year), and Jason Robards in 1922. I haven't selected these people, I am putting them down as they appear in the *Horoscope* book, and I thank the editors and

publishers and all. It doesn't make my work any easier, and does perhaps make it at least slightly more confusing, but it is nice to have it all laid out that way, that way, don't you know. Rembrandt was an Armenian, the Armenians say. This helps of course, but only as it helps anybody at all, not just Armenians, for it has been disputed and proved that even though there is evidence that he was, there is also evidence that he wasn't. He was born, that's all. And so were you. Forget it. Skip it. Let it go. I forget. I even forget what I dreamed last night, and what a loss that must be to you, Oh friend in the future, as Walter Whitman would say, or Mr. Walter Whitman had he also been an executive at a bank or at an insurance company, like T. S. Eliot and Wallace Stevens. Everybody who writes a poem isn't necessarily a bum, you know? Some of the boys settle themselves into chairs of responsibility and even authority. God bless them, and you, is all I can say. God really really really bless them.
12:25 P.M